A GUIDE TO PROFITABLE HYDROPONICS

PREFACE

There is a plethora of information now available on the internet, much of it contributed by amateurs or would-be hobbyists, and not all of it accurate. The result is a confusing melee of information.

The fact is that hydroponics may be practised using a wide variety of systems and growing media, which in itself merely adds to the confusion, so students and aspirant growers often possess the equivalent of a fishing 'overwind' in their heads when they first start out.

Disentangling this mix-up often costs heavy school fees as they find out the best ways of doing things by trial and error.

This book seeks to eliminate that situation by suggesting proven, uncomplicated and cost-effective ways of doing things in hydroponics.

ABOUT THE AUTHOR

Brought up on a farm in KwaZulu-Natal, South Africa,, John Sandison spent most of his working life with two International Industrial Companies at senior level, both abroad and in South Africa.

Trained originally in Business Management in Birmingham and London he then spent time in Argentina and Spain before returning to Johannesburg.

He retired from industrial management at aged 55 and returned to KwaZulu-Natal to start up a strawberry farm which eventually boasted over 220 000 strawberry plants. Unfortunately, the hot and humid climate, exacerbated by global warming, became too much for the strawberries and along with eight others, the farm closed.

With 12 years' experience in hydroponics, growing strawberries and other types of fresh produce, and backed by academic knowledge, a sideways shift into consultancy and education was inevitable. Thus the DaisyFresh Hydroponic School was born, and courses have been given to more than 200 delegates over 8 years.

John holds certificates in Business Management and Advanced Hydroponics. He and his wife retired to Warwick, UK.

HOW TO USE THIS BOOK

The various topics concerning hydroponics and hydroponic related items and systems have been segmented and are dealt with in Chapters starting with History of Hydroponics and Definitions and followed by Electrical Conductivity (EC), pH (measures acidity and alkalinity) and parts per million(ppm's). The segments are corralled into Chapters and, after learning how to measure the strength of nutrient solutions and their pH, which is primordial to just about all aspects of hydroponics, the Chapters are put into virtually a random order.

You may choose to read the book like a novel, going from front to back. However, we have ensured that it has a useful Index at the back that covers every possible aspect that may arise as a query, so you may find it more useful to use as a reference book, going straight to the subject of your query to get the answers you seek. Whichever method you choose is up to your own personal preference.

CONTENTS

CHAPTER ONE
WHAT IS HYDROPONICS?

It's important at the outset to know exactly what it is and, of course, how it works. It is a science all of its own, part chemistry part agriculture and is the growing of plants in a solution of water-soluble minerals without any soil. The fact that no soil is present is the distinguishing factor between hydro-ponics and traditional agriculture as many of the other ancillary factors are common to both disciplines.

In traditional soil-based agriculture the soil supplies the nutrients to the plant whereas in hydroponics nutrition comes from the nutrient water and can also come from foliar sprays applied for additional growth where this is deemed necessary. In hydroponics the growing medium anchors the plant and gives it stability and provides a degree of buffering capacity by keeping the roots moist between feeds. Growing media are sterile and do not supply any nutrients to the plants.

CHAPTER TWO
HISTORY OF HYDROPONICS

Source::Wikipedia; Maarten van Heemskerk

Hanging Gardens of Babylon

The earliest recorded history of hydroponics is thought to have been the 'Hanging Gardens of Babylon' but this is not so, simply because in ancient Babylon they had no compound chemicals nor water soluble ones, so were unable to feed their plants with nutrient water. The Hanging Gardens were at best a series of potted plants at various levels where water was channelled through a series of descending pipes and gutters to cleverly encompass each plant on its way to the lower levels. Soil-less growing of cultivated plants actually began in the 1930s as an outgrowth of the culture techniques used by plant physiologists in plant nutrition experiments in the USA. During World War II, for example, several U.S. Army units successfully produced vegetables hydroponically at various overseas bases. Vitamin C is an important ingredient of the human diet, without which the human body can get scurvy as happened during the 16th Century when sailing ships spent long periods away from land and the source of fresh vegetables. The lack of vitamins causes various ill-effects on human health. Thus, the US army was able to over¬come the lack of fresh vegetables for the troops by growing them hydroponically in the South Pacific by using the availability of plenty of white beach sand together with fresh mountain streams coming from the volcanic islands. One can easily understand the great need that the US army must have had to have fresh vegetables on hand to feed the troops. In the early forties air travel was still very slow and a trip from the closest state, California, to the South Sea Islands would have taken at least two days, and this time would have had to be added onto picking, packing and transport time to the airbases.

 In the 1960s hydroponic farming developed on a commercial scale in the arid regions of the United States, particularly in Arizona, where research was also undertaken at state universities. In other arid regions, such as Israel, the Persian Gulf and the Arab oil-producing states, hydroponic farming of tomatoes and cucumbers is under way.
These countries are also researching an additional group of crops that may be grown by this method, as they have limited arable land, but plenty of sand and clean water from the underground water table.

CHAPTER THREE
DEFINITIONS

To help one fully understand hydroponics and the surrounding inputs to it an organigram of the players is reproduced here:

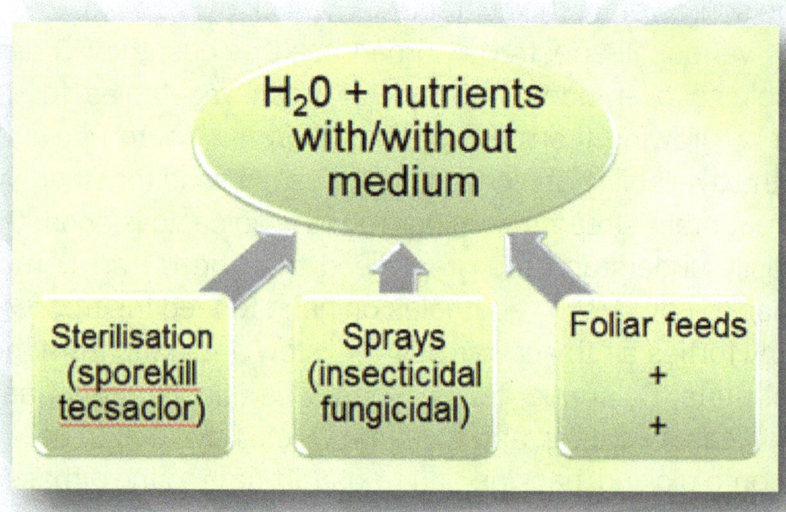

Source: DaisyFresh Hydroponics

One can see from the diagram that the nutrient water is applied to the plants either with a medium or without one.

Plants can even hang in the air and their roots sprayed with nutrient water from below. This is Aeroponics which will be dealt with later.

Plants are fed by a carefully controlled nutrient solution, with no nutrition coming from the growing medium.

The nutrient water must be kept sterilised at all times to ensure that it is pathogen-free and this is especially important if the plants are exposed to the rain as rain-vectored pathogenic spores may enter the root zones of the plants and infect them.

Either Sporekill (didecyldimethylammonium chloride) or Tecsaclor (chlorine dioxide) are effective sterilisation agents which can be added to the nutrient water, and a UV light sterilisation unit can also be added to the nutrient feed line as a double precaution against pathogens. Action also must be taken to keep the upper structure of the plant free of insects and diseases, so insecticidal and fungicidal sprays should be applied to the leaves, along with growth hormones and growth stimulants to maximise the yields of the plants. These can be chemical based, but so much progress has been made with biological remedies in recent years that it is preferable to apply these remedies as they are user-friendly, unlike many of the toxic chemical sprays used in yesteryear.

In recent years Israel has made great strides with hydroponic innovation and ranks as a world leader in hydroponic supplies along with USA and Australia. Currently, Israel can manufacture a four part extruded tunnel-cover capable of covering tunnels 10m in width, and their technology in the construction of multispan growing houses is also very superior.
The word 'hydroponics' is derived from the Greek 'ponos' meaning to work and 'hydro' meaning water, from which we would derive the sense of working in water.

The Latin verb 'ponere' meaning to place could also contribute to the meaning to place in water. Either way it should not be confused with HYDROPHONICS which is the sound water makes, or sounds made under water.

CHAPTER FOUR
DIVISIONS

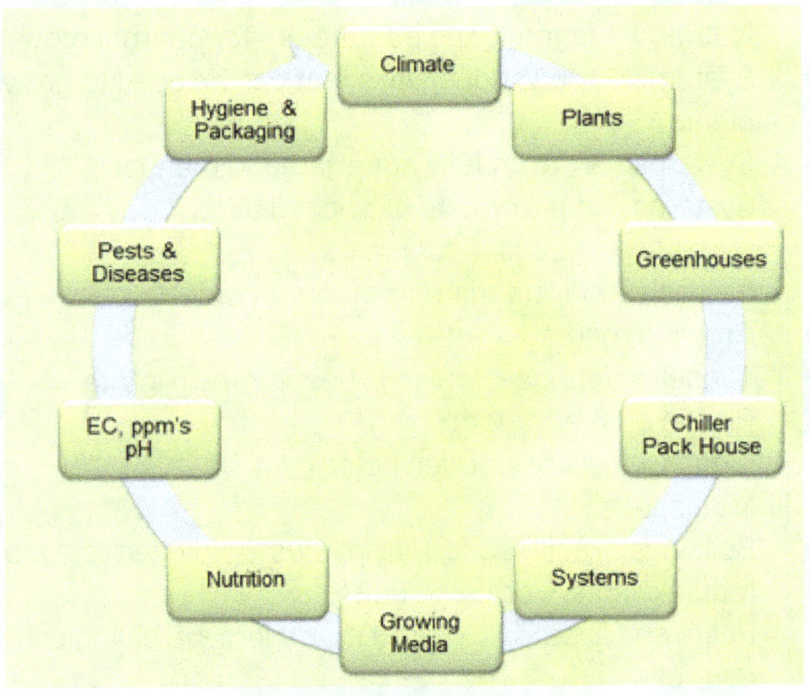

Source: DaisyFresh Hydroponics

Hydroponics is divided up into two parts:

Part 1 -Basic or intrinsic hydroponics:
learning how to operate and grow successfully

Part 2 - Applications in Hydroponics – polishing up and furthering your knowledge to maximise yields and profits through further reading.

Part 1 - Basic hydroponics consists of the following subdivisions:
- Plants, plant physiology, learning how they work
- EC, ppm's and pH – what they mean and how to use them
- Nutrition – learning the parameters for optimal growth
- Systems – the various ways that can be used to grow plants
- Systems ¬¬– from fully automated to manual
- Systems – run to waste or re-circulating
- Climatic preferences for plants
- Site Selection, criteria for optimum yields
- Growing media
- Tunnel coverings – which is best for the climate
  i. Plastic or shade cloth
  ii. Metal tunnels or wooden poles
  iii. Multispans
- Buildings -Pack house, Pump house and chemical store requirements – do's and don'ts
- Pests and Diseases – good management, biological controls
- Organics – how to be organic - hydroponic
- Marketing
- Hygiene and Packaging
- Transportation
- Global Gap
- Setting a Breakeven Point for Your Business

Part 2 - Applications in Hydroponics

- Cost-effective hydroponics
- How Hydroponics Saves Water
- How Hydroponics Works
- How to Erect Your Own Greenhouse, Simply and Economically.
- How to Grow Produce in a Hot, Humid Climate
- Hydroponics – a Solution for the Water Shortage
- Hydroponics Training – Why it's Important
- Pitfalls in Hydroponics
- Save Money by Growing Your Own Vegetables
- The 'Breathing' Greenhouse Concept

PART 1
BASIC HYDROPONICS

CHAPTER FIVE
PLANTS, PLANT PHYSIOLOGY, LEARNING HOW THEY WORK

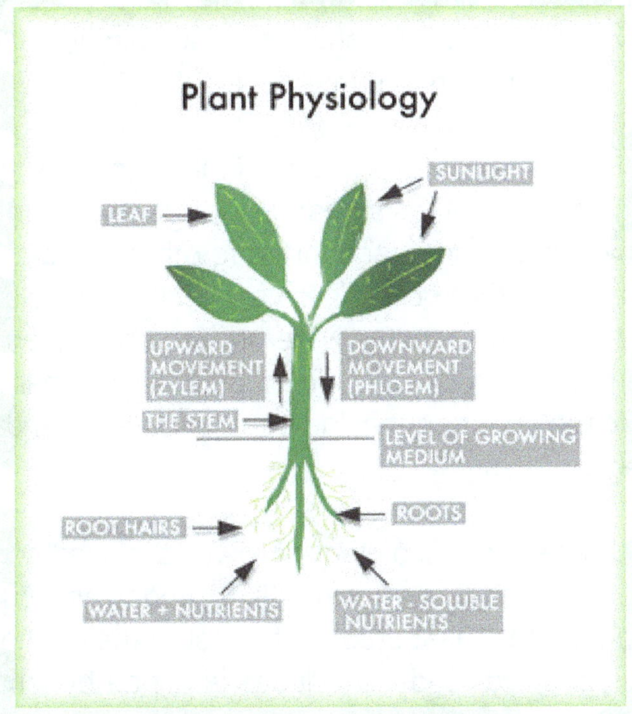

Source: DaisyFresh Hydroponics

The plant consists of three main sections: the roots, the stem and the leaves. The roots anchor the plant in the medium and small root hairs are responsible for the absorption of the nutrients which takes place through osmosis. Without water osmosis cannot take place so nutrients cannot get into the plant which then suffers from malnutrition, the first signs of which are wilting leaves. Of course without water, transpiration also cannot take place with similar resultant effects.

The plant is really a factory. It takes in light through the leaves and through photosynthesis changes it into energy in the form of sugars which are then transported to other areas of the plant like the stem and the roots. There are some parallels between plants' and humans' vascular systems. The arteries and veins in humans are mirrored by the phloem and the xylem in the plant which carry the sugar-containing sap downwards and upwards respectively.

There are three stages to a plant's growth: the seed and germination, the seedling and growth, flowering and fruiting. The prime purpose of the last stage is to ensure the continuation of the species and the food it produces is a side benefit for man and animals.

The plants' nutrient requirements change as it passes from one stage to the next and this must be borne in mind by the grower who will need to adjust his nutrient mix accordingly. See section on Nutrition.

Thus, the plant factory's raw materials are:
- Light
- Nutrition (in the form of minerals)
- Water
- Gases (carbon, oxygen and hydrogen)

Without any of these, or with reduced quantities of them, the plant will suffer and not perform to its maximum ability. This is important to bear in mind if one is to extract maximum yields from the plants and should not be forgotten when designing systems or selecting a site for the hydroponic project.

See Site Selection, Criteria for Optimum Yields

CHAPTER SIX
EC, PPMS AND PH – WHAT THEY MEAN AND HOW TO USE THEM.

EC stands for Electrical Conductivity and in the case of nutrient water, is measured in Siemens per cm, named after the German Scientist, Werner Von Siemens. The principle of using an electrical conductivity charge is based on the valence of each element as laid out in the basic table of elements. Thus each mineral salt will contribute its natural ability to conduct electricity to the overall conductivity of the sum total of all the elements in a given nutrient mix or cocktail of elements. The greater the concentration of nutrient salts in a solution, the higher will be its EC. Distilled or non-ionised water will have an EC of 0, simply because it contains zero presence of conducting minerals.

Experience, and a reference to specialist hydroponic manuals, will enable the hydroponic farmer to set the EC level for the particular crop that he is growing. Each crop will show a different EC level preference, and within each crop, a different EC level will have to be used for the various stages of a plant's growth, from small seedling to fully grown plant, through to the fruiting or bearing stage. One should also know the limit for any plant beyond which leaf burn will occur, as this too varies from plant type to plant type. As an example, it's useful to know that the leaf burn limit for strawberries is 1.8 EC, beyond which plants will exhibit leaf burn symptoms irrespective of cultivar type, time of year, and stage of growth or fruiting development. Beans on the other hand, require an optimal nutritional level of 4.0 EC when starting to grow, cutting back to 2.0 EC when fully-grown and about to bear fruit. See Reference Section for recommended books giving EC levels.

There is an obvious correlation between EC and parts per million (ppm's), which is another way to measure the concentration of nutrients in a solution. The latter expresses the weight in grams (gm) of an element relative to a million parts of water measured in cubic centimetres (cc's). Therefore, the concentration of a nutrient solution expressed in ppm's will be the sum of all its individual elements' ppm's.

There is a constant average ratio between these two methods of measuring nutrient concentration. Thus, we can convert ppm's to EC and vice versa simply by applying this constant ratio, which is 200. So if one were to take an EC of say, 1.5 and convert it to ppms 1.5 x 200 = 300ppms. And if one had a solution of 550 ppms and wanted to know what EC that would equate to, one would divide 550 by 200 which would give an EC of 2.75.

It's a good idea to acquire a good quality EC/pH/TDS meter. There are many different models on the market, especially those made in China, which tend to be singular meters only capable of measuring either EC or pH but not both. There is a model available that measures both with a single meter that also incorporates temperature measurement made by Hanna Instruments.

This is very handy, apart from the obvious cost-saving when it comes time to replace the probe which can be separated from the meter body itself, so both probe and meter do not have to be replaced together. Having such a multi-meter saves considerable time and money by not having to carry three or four meters around and hop from one to the next. The downside is that the investment is high, but not as high as purchasing four separate meters.

The probe of the multi-meter should never be allowed to dry out so it's a good idea to procure a plastic jar and saw a hole in the lid to fit the probe. By filling the jar half-full of water, the probe can rest in it while measurements are being taken. Before putting the probe away always ensure that it is dipped in storage solution which will help to extend its useful life.

The meters can tend to go out of calibration from time to time so it's a good idea to check the calibration regularly. This can be done every two weeks or more often if it's suspected that a reading is incorrect. Calibration solution is available from equipment or laboratory suppliers. Check the list of suppliers at the back of this book.

Water soluble fertiliser manufacturers often state the ppm content of the minerals on the exterior of the fertiliser bag. In any case the ppm levels of these minerals are always available from them along with their recommended ratios for mixing.
pH stands for 'pouvoir hydrogène' which is French for the 'power of hydrogen' and comprises the negative logarithm of the numbers of Hydrogen ions (protons) present in a solution, liquid or water.

The pH of water or any solution is expressed as a number between 0 and 14 with 7.0 being neutral.

Any value above 7.0 would indicate that the solution is alkaline and any value below 7.0 would indicate an acidic solution. The pH value of nutritional water is important because it affects the degree of uptake of a particular mineral.

Water pH from Municipalities tends to be alkalinic and can be as high as 10 or more so acid has to be added to the water to bring the pH down to the optimal level for Hydroponics which is between 5.5 and 6.0. The recommended acid for this purpose is Phosphoric because it causes the least amount of conversion work that the plant must perform.

Should the pH be below 5.5 for any reason (such as over acidification in error) then an alkalinic agent such as Calcium Hydroxide needs to be added. Do this by trial and error using very small amounts at a time as it has a high buffering capacity and a little goes a very long way. CaOH is available from laboratory supplies companies or from chemical companies if large quantities are required. Do take care when handling either acid or alkalines as they are both corrosive and damage to unprotected skin and eyes can result. Make sure that goggles, gloves and overalls are worn when handling these two rascals.

CHAPTER SEVEN
NUTRITION – LEARN THE PARAMETERS FOR OPTIMAL GROWTH

Plant nutrition has many parallels with mammalian nutrition and basically covers the principle that living organisms require sustenance for growth, development and survival. The nutritional levels should most closely approximate what the plant will remove from the mix to satisfy its needs.

Science has determined that plants require 16 elements for growth (although increasingly, other elements in very small amounts are now found to be desirable, such as, for example, Silica (Si) Chromium (Cr) and Selenium (Si)). These trace elements are used in such minute amounts that they are barely measurable and are not therefore classified as nutrients in the accepted sense. Nutrients are supplied from air, water and fertilisers. The 16 elements are:

Gases: Carbon (C), Hydrogen (H), Oxygen (O), - supplied from the air

Six Macro nutrients: Calcium (Ca), Magnesium (Mg), Nitrogen (N), Phosphorous (P), Potassium (K), Sulphur (S

Seven Micro nutrients: Boron (B), Chlorine (Cl) Copper (Cu), Iron (Fe), Manganese (Mn), Molybdenum (Mo), and Zinc (Zn)

The key to successful management of a fertiliser programme is to ensure adequate concentrations of all nutrients throughout the life cycle of the crop. Inadequate or excessive amounts of any nutrient result in poor performance of the crop. Excessive amounts can be especially troublesome since they can damage the crop, waste money and fertiliser resources, and pollute the environment when fertiliser is released during flushing of the nutrient delivery system.

How does one decide how many waterings to give the plants to achieve optimal nutrition?

In bag or pot culture where the growing medium possesses a degree of moisture retentive capacity, the plants are not as sensitive to the presence or lack of water. In summer when temperatures are high the transpiration rate of the plants increases so more waterings are required, and in winter the converse is true. A simple low-cost moisture meter will indicate whether the medium is dry or wet. As a rough guide waterings should be at least 5 in summer and three in winter. First watering should take place at sunrise, and last watering at 3 p.m. as the plant's requirements for nutrition close down by then.

A more precise and scientific approach to nutrition and watering is available in the form of 'on demand nutrient dosing'. This electronic device measures the EC and water content in the bag or growing pot and according to pre-set parameters will command the fertigation equipment to feed the plants when moisture levels have dropped to levels requiring a top-up. The level of water will be high during rainy periods, so it has a built-in fail-safe parameter that checks the EC levels as well.

If these are low as would be the case with rain the fertigation equipment is still activated so that the plants are still fed nutrient rich water despite the rain. The nutrient feed displaces the rain water. The results of this method of scientific plant fertigation are highly desirable and can produce maximum yields at minimum consumption of nutrients and water, both expensive and precious resources. This is an essential tool to calculate precisely how much water the plants require and can increase yields by as much as 100% whilst lowering consumption of nutrients and water by as much as 50% at the same time.

It is possible to mix one's own nutrients by purchasing the various compounds and scientifically mixing the right amounts together to provide a balanced, but not equal, fertiliser programme. Small savings can be made by doing this, as one would be eliminating this part of the working activity that nutrient fertiliser suppliers do. However, to do this has so many downsides that it's not to be recommended. Firstly, if you use industrial grade fertilisers you cannot guarantee that they will be free of impurities. You don't need anything that could be a threat to clogging your dripper system. It is work enough for one to keep them clean and unblocked without this extra threat. Secondly, one runs the risk of making an error in mixing and weighing because of yet another step in the many task-filled days that running a successful hydroponicum takes. More activities = more chances of mistakes creeping in. Most fertiliser companies supply a cocktail mix of macro and micro nutrients ready-mixed in the right proportions for your plants. They will supply the $CaNo_3$ separately as Ca and S when mixed together react to form $CaSo_4$, which is gypsum (or ceiling board).

In other words, they set-up when allowed to come into contact with one another. It's a bit like epoxy resin when you mix the base and the catalyst together. Rather, find out from fertiliser suppliers which water-soluble nutrients are recommended from their range for a particular crop and stick with that. Use the supplier lists at the back of this book and shop around. Prices vary significantly from one supplier to another.

How do manufacturers arrive at the particular ratio of macro and micro nutrients that they supply?

There are potentially thousands of different hydroponic nutrient formulations or 'recipes' which have been published and are currently being used for crop production. There are also many different schools of thought when it comes to what constitutes the best nutrient formulation for various crops. What is most interesting however, is that ever since the very early days of hydroponics, nutrient formulation components have not changed that much. We do have more modern fertilisers such as chelates, and greater purity of some fertiliser salts, but the main ingredients of hydroponic formulations are still fairly much the same as was used back in the 1930s. What has changed are the ratios and amounts of nutrient ions we aim to maintain in solution – largely because of advances in plant nutritional research which has given us valuable information about nutrient uptake and because of the modern cultivars used in crop production these days which have vastly superior growth rates and yields to those available back in the 1930s.

One thing that all nutrient formulas have in common is that they aim to supply the plant with all the essential elements required in ratios close to what the plant will remove from the nutrient. This then means that a nutrient formula not only supplies all of the plant's requirements, so that no toxicity or deficiency in any one element occurs, but also that ions are removed from the solution in the ratios in which they are continually supplied. So over time, the nutrient solution does not become imbalanced with higher rates of some ions than others, and this will maximise the useful life of the nutrient solution. The following table outlines the range for each element commonly used in hydroponic formulations. For some elements there is a relatively wide range as different crops have different requirements and uptake rates.

Common elemental ranges in hydroponic formulations:

Element	ppms
Nitrogen (N)	100-450
Phosphorus (P)	10-100
Potassium (K)	100-750
Magnesium (Mg)	20-95
Calcium (Ca)	70-350
Sulphur (S)	20-250
Iron (Fe)	1-6
Manganese (Mn)	0.8-4
Boron (B)	0.3-0.8
Zinc (Zn)	0.2-0.5
Copper (Cu)	0.05-0.1
Molybdenum (Mo)	0.02-0.07

To give one an idea of the proportions each element contributes to the total mix the ppm's of a typical blend, plus Calcium Nitrate and CalMag +B is reproduced as follows:

	GROMOR		NUTRIENT SOLUTION
	New Generation Coastal Blend + micros	Calmag N + micros	1kg new Generation Coastal Blend + 1kg Calmag N + micros in 1000 litres water
	g/kg	g/kg	g/1000 litres (ppm)
N	62	148	210 (89% nitrate 11% ammonia)
P	44	Nil	44
K	245	Nil	245
Ca	Nil	177	177
Mg	14	14	28
S	79	Nil	79
	mg/kg	mg/kg	mg/1000 litres
Fe	689	700	1389
Mn	229	161	390
Zn	273	141	414
Cu	14	18	32
B	442	210	652
Mo	91	28	119

Source: National Plant Food

Complexities of the various cocktail blends aside it is very important that the nutritional elements are supplied to the plants in the correct proportions. There are parallels with human nutrition in this regard. Just as a human diet should consist of a balanced amount of carbohydrates, proteins, amino acids,

essential fatty acids, minerals and vitamins so the plants
nutritional elements should also be balanced.
The following are the prescribed ratios of four of the most pivotal
macro nutrients. The minerals must fall within these ratios if
nutritional problems are to be avoided. If a supplier's mix does
not fall within these ratios then it is better to avoid that mixture
and seek an alternative and balanced source of supply.

    N : K   0,06 - 1,25 : 1
    K : Ca   1 - 2 : 1
    Ca : Mg   2,5 - 5 : 1

Nutritional problems can arise if these ratios are not adhered to
because of what is known as Symbiosis and Antithesis which
is alternatively referred to as Stimulation and Antagonism. This
can more readily be understood if one thinks of the minerals as
having friends and enemies.

Certain elements can be regarded as catalysts and the uptake of
certain other nutrients by the plants is increased in their
presence. This is known as symbiosis. Conversely, certain
other elements inhibit the uptake of certain other elements by
their presence and this is known as antithesis or antagonism.

The following chart demonstrates which elements inhibit the
uptake of which other elements and which ones encourage the
uptake of which other elements:

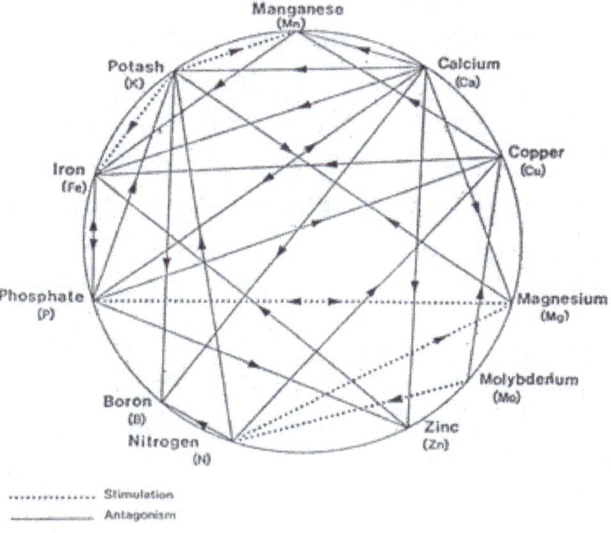

Source: ACS Distance Education

As mentioned earlier nutrient formulas aim to supply the plant with the essential elements in ratios close to what the plant will remove from the solution so that ions are removed from the solution in the ratios in which they are continually supplied. How does one establish then, what ratios the plant requires of all the individual nutrients throughout its life cycle to ensure that supply matches demand? Fortunately, much work over the years has already been done to establish this and most crops have been analysed at the various stages of their growth cycles and the results published in a book by *REUTER AND ROBINSON*

Having established what should be found within the crops' cells the next question that concerns the grower is what levels of nutrients are actually found within his crop's leaves? Naturally it's important to establish how closely the grower's nutritional programme is in supplying what the plant needs. A disparity will result in toxicity or deficiency symptoms which, in turn, will manifest in depressed yields. Most Depts. of Agriculture maintain laboratories where leaf analyses are undertaken so it's important to take a plastic bag full of the most recent adult leaves to the lab for analysis. Omnia Fertilisers also undertake sap analyses for a reasonable fee. Their results are published in a unique way which the following table will demonstrate.

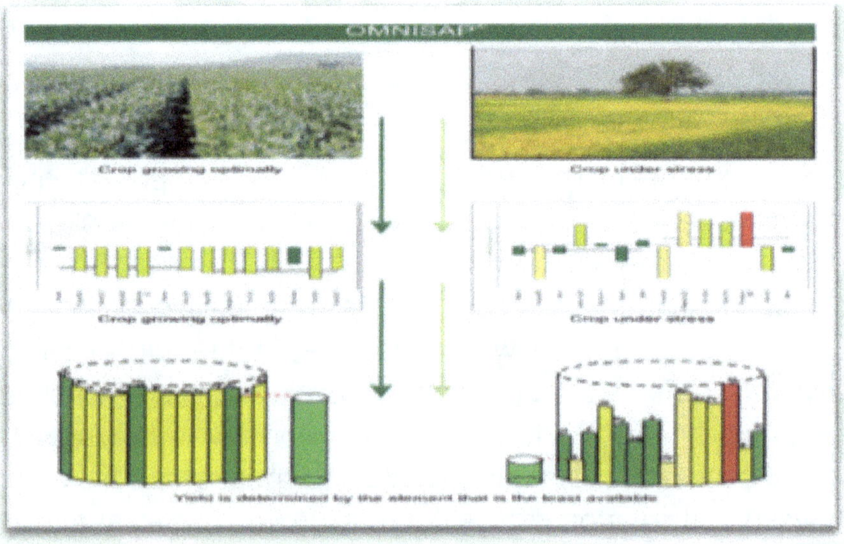

Source: Omnia Fertilisers Ltd

The central horizontal line on the bar charts represents the optimal nutritional ratio relating to that mineral. Bar charts above the line show adequate quantities of nutrient while those below the line show deficiencies in them. Red indicates toxicity. These positive and negative values are converted into a barrel chart to graphically represent, among the others, the lowest mineral present. Nutrient uptake of all minerals is governed by and reduced to the value of the lowest contributor. Thus, it matters not whether 12 of the 13 elements are at par, their uptake will be reduced to the level of the lowest value and this is shown clearly in the comparison between the two crops in the photographs.

When the results are published compare them with the nominal levels contained in Reuter and Robinson and make any adjustments necessary. Deficiencies can be remedied by adding small amounts of chelated minerals but this action should only be taken as a last resort as it could upset the delicate balance between stimulation and antagonism and the prescribed ratios. Rather, check the pH level first to see whether it could be playing a part.

In 1947 a man named Truog working for the US Dept. of Agriculture discovered that different elements were taken up by plants faster or slower depending upon the pH level of the solution, and he published his findings in the form of a table, as follows:

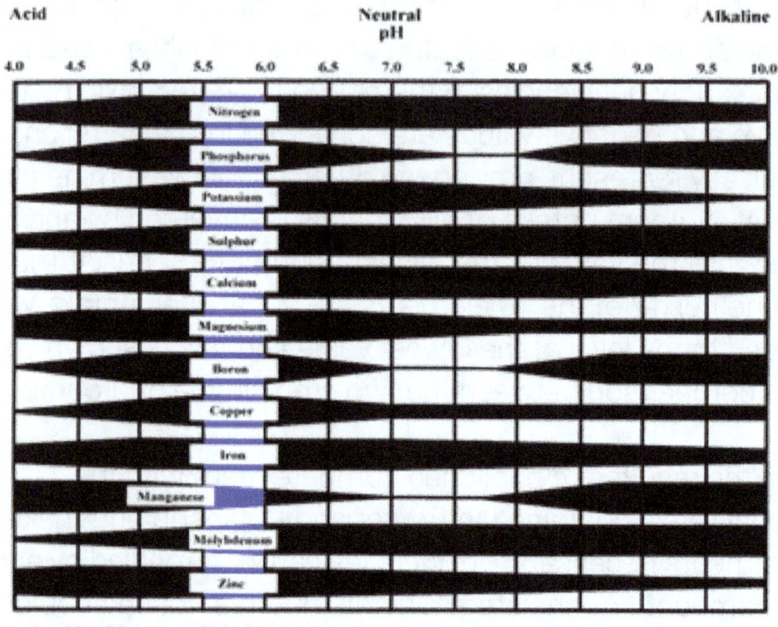

Source: ACS Distance Learning

From this it can be appreciated that if pH levels are outside the 'compromise' range of 5.5 – 6.0 the uptake of specific minerals could be severely affected which in most cases accounts for any disparity between nominal and actual nutrient levels.

Most **soils** are indicated for optimal nutrient uptake when the pH is somewhere between 6.0 and 6.5 whereas with **hydroponic media** the optimal pH reading for maximum nutrient uptake is between 5.5 and 6.0, which is slightly more acidic.

Hydroponic farm management requires meticulous attention to detail, so some focus also needs to be given to the nutrient levels being supplied to the plants. It's one thing for the fertiliser supplier to mix the blends in the required ratios but quite another for the nutrient solution arriving at the drippers to be at the correct EC, pH and mineral ratios. It's a good idea to compare the nutrient levels in the tank/s with the manufacturers' specifications and the EC levels with the plant recommendations. The plant EC recommendations can be ascertained by reference to various reference books on the subject including "Commercial Hydroponics" by John Mason. Water samples of raw water, and nutrient solution at the dripper outlets, should be taken periodically to a lab or Dept. of Agriculture for actual analysis and comparison with the recommended levels.

Some labs, especially Dept. Agriculture, publish the analysis results in milli-equivalents. Should the lab analysis results of the nutrient water analysis be expressed in this form one will need to convert these values into ppm's for them to make sense. This conversion is different for each mineral as milli-equivalents is a chemistry term which is derived from the molecular weight of each individual element and its valance. There are tables of conversion factors in some hydroponic nutrient formulation software to convert to ppm, which will do this process automatically: Here are the manual conversion factors:

It is important to emphasise, when comparing leaf analysis results, that these should be compared with what ideally should be in the leaves and not with the ratios of elements found in the nutrient water analysis.

From	To	Multiply by
meq/l N-NO3 or N-NH4	ppm N	14
meq/l H2PO4	ppm P	31
meq/l K (Potassium)	ppm K	39
meq/l Ca (Calcium)	ppm Ca	20
meq/l Mg (Magnesium	ppm Mg	12
meq/l SO4 (Sulfate)	ppm SO4	48
meq/l Na (Sodium)	ppm Na	23
meq/l Cl (Chloride)	ppm Cl	35.5

From	To	Multiply by
ppm N-NO3 or N-NH4	meq/l N	0.07143
ppm P (Phosphorus)	meq/l H2PO4	0.03226
ppm K (Potassium)	meq/l K	0.0256
ppm Ca (Calcium)	meq/l Ca	0.05
ppm Mg (Magnesium)	meq/l Mg	0.0833
ppm SO4 (Sulfate)	meq/l SO4	0.02083
ppm Na (Sodium)	meq/l Na	0.04348
ppm C1 (Chlorides)	meq/l Cl	0.02817

The tank water analysis should approximate what the fertiliser manufacturer specifies his ratios are, and the fertiliser company should be manufacturing the minerals in accordance with the values mentioned earlier

CHAPTER EIGHT
CLIMATIC PREFERENCES FOR PLANTS

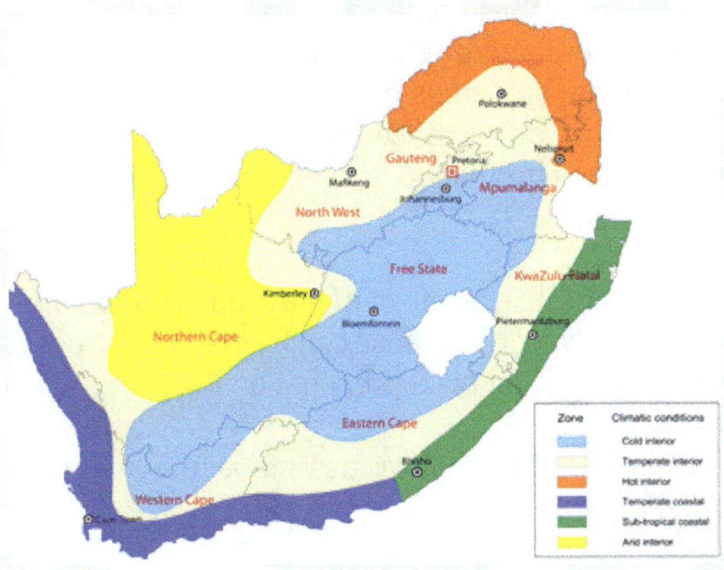

Map source: Google Maps

Whilst it may appear obvious that different plants prefer different climates the specifics of these preferences can be easily overlooked. For example, strawberries cannot just be grown anywhere as their preference is for 'cool and dry'. That means, looking at the foregoing map, that they cannot be grown in hot and sub-tropical areas at all and can only be grown in winter in the temperate areas. Conversely, vanilla can only be grown in hot or subtropical areas. There are reasons why nothing grows at the poles, and only certain plants can grow in the tropics, why some plants prefer humid climates and others dry ones.

The fact that the plant is grown hydroponically and not in the ground makes no difference to its climatic preferences; as mentioned earlier the only difference between the two methods of growing is the plant's nutrition and its source.

It follows therefore that some careful study should be made of plant preferences before embarking on a hydroponic growing project. There are numerous gardening books available that list these preferences or reference these days can be made to the internet as much information is to be found there, but not all of it accurate.

Every country has its equivalent of the map found on the previous page to which reference can be made when deciding on appropriate choices for plant propagation.

Here are some pointers that will assist one to make the appropriate choice:

Warm Loving Plants (can stand no frost):

	Preferred Temps. C
Beans	15 - 21
Capsicum Peppers	21 - 24
Chillies	21 - 29
Cucumber	18 - 24
Egg Plant	21 - 29
Granadilla	21 - 29
Marrow	18 - 24
Okra	21 - 29
Patty Pan Pumpkins	18 - 24
Pumpkin	18 - 24

Rock melon	18 - 24
Squash	18 - 24
Sweet potato	21 - 29
Tomato	21 - 24
Zuccini	18 - 24

Temperate Loving Plants:
(for warm areas in winter and temperate areas in summer)

Chicory	13 - 24
Chives	13 - 24
Garlic	13 - 24
Gem Squash	18 - 24
Ginger	18 - 24
Hubbard Squash	18 - 24
Leek	13 - 24
Onion	13 - 24
Shallot	13 - 24
Spring Onions	13 - 24

Cool Loving Plants: (for temperate areas in winter)

Artichoke	15 - 18
Beetroot	15 - 18
Broccoli	15 - 18
Brussel Sprouts	15 - 18
Cabbage	15 - 18
Carrots	15 - 18
Cauliflower	15 - 18
Celery	15 - 18
Coriander	15 - 18
Endive	15 - 18
Fennel	15 - 18

Horseradish	15 - 18
Kale	15 - 18
Kohlrabi	15 - 18
Lettuce	15 - 18
Mustard	15 - 18
Pak-Choi	15 - 18
Radish	15 - 18
Parsley	15 - 18
Pea	15 - 18
Potatoes	15 - 18
Radish	15 - 18
Rhubarb	15 - 18
Silver Beet	15 - 18
Spinach	15 - 18
Swedes	15 - 18
Swiss Chard	15 - 18
Turnip	15 - 18

Cold Loving Plants: (for cold areas and temperate areas in winter)

All berries

CHAPTER NINE
CULTIVATING THE RIGHT PRODUCE

The decision on what produce to cultivate does not rest solely on which produce grows best in the area one has in mind. Other factors need to be considered such as the demand profile in the area.

A thorough study of the demand should be undertaken through visits to the local shops, restaurants, wholesalers and supermarket retailers to establish what is in short supply and when, and whether you will be able to satisfy the shortfall. Conversely if there is an oversupply of an item in the area it would be best to delay production until a later more favourable time. It's no good deciding to grow lettuce for example, and then find that there is a surfeit of it on the local markets and it can't even be given away.

Perhaps one could supply the local supermarket. Pay them a visit and establish what their needs are and assess the competition. Always try and supply what others are not supplying. To supply one of the Big Five supermarket retailers one will first have to set up the hydroponicum to GLOBAL GAP standards (refer Chapter 23). These are onerous, and the cost of an audit is between \$400 and \$650, depending upon how many lines are grown. Pay these outlets a visit and establish what their needs are and assess the competition. Always try and supply what others are not supplying.

The upside is that the retailers can move vast quantities of produce which will take a single daily delivery. They generally pay better prices than the public markets and one can sometimes arrange prompt payment terms with them. The downside is that they will often act as though they own one; they insist on hygiene laboratory tests at the supplier's expense and they never guarantee offtake quantities. The quantities they order can vary wildly and there's no guarantee that they'll not drop a supplier without warning, leaving the supplier, his staff and his company high and dry. Be warned! Supplying a national retailer is not all plain sailing. Before deciding on which system you'd like to choose for your hydroponic system you need to decide what type of vegetable or fruit you want to grow. For example, for growing carrots, the most suitable system is sand beds, while strawberries are grown most cost-effectively in vertical growing systems (provided the cold requirements of the plants are first met) whilst lettuce and celery are suited to growing vertically or in NFT systems.

Once one has established to whom one is going to sell the produce and what they want, only then can one decide what to grow. In this little exercise, don't overlook flowers.

Never forget that hydroponic nutrients are expensive, making it unviable to grow low-cost produce like spinach that receive only pennies a bunch at the local municipal market. The higher the price per item of produce the more viable will the operation be. So, concentrate first on *high value high volume items.*

CHAPTER TEN
SYSTEMS – THE VARIOUS WAYS THAT CAN BE USED TO GROW PLANTS

Nutrient Film Technique:

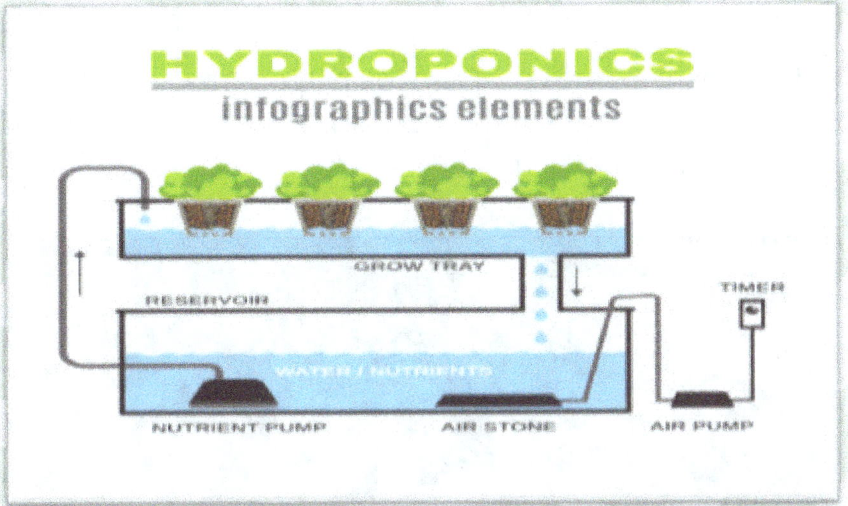

Source: Dreamstime.com

NFT is very popular with hydroponic growers all over the world and is a widely used method comprising a gutter-like channel (usually PVC) covered over with a lid having holes placed at optimal intervals into which the seedlings are placed. The base of the channel is usually covered with a coir or fibrous matting to help spread the nutrient solution evenly across the channel width to form a film.

The channel is set at a slight slope so that the nutrient solution can run down it and away, either into a
collection tank for re-cycling or run-to-waste. Running-to-waste is very expensive as nutrients are no longer cheap.
It is far preferable to collect the leachate (used nutrient water) and pump it back to the header tank for subsequent re-use and by so doing save on both water and nutrients.

The NFT channels are usually set on purpose made trestle tables so that they are at a convenient waist height for ease of accessibility and working.

Source: © Kenishirotie | Dreamstime.com

Gravel Bed Technique:

Sunken Gravel Beds

The use of gravel beds is another popular technique; beds can be built easily by placing a row of bricks in a long rectangular layout and placing a thick black sheet of PVC over it, into which 8-10 mm gravel stones are then poured. The thickness of the gravel bed needs to be no more than the depth to which the roots will grow, but shallow enough to enable them to reach the nutrient as it flows through. This is a relatively cheap and easy method of construction and again, the nutrient can be easily collected by means of a drainage pipe and a suitably sized tank.

Gravel beds are good for growing lettuces, spinach, cabbages, cauliflowers, and broccoli.

Gravel beds can be constructed either by digging the bed out of the earth, lining it with a suitable 450-micron hydro liner, and then filling it in with the gravel stones, or alternatively by building a two-brick high surrounding wall and covering that with the hydro liner and gravel stones. Perhaps the most effective way of gravel bed construction is to use gum poles one on top of the other and keep them in position with mild steel fence droppers cut to length. Also, instead of using expensive hydro liner, SABS 250-micron plastic sheeting, doubled over, can be used.

A combination of gravel beds and shadecloth held in position by gum poles makes an economic hydroponic set up that is accessible for both the hobbyist and commercial grower. Another advantage of this method is that it is modular and can be extended easily.

The main disadvantage of gravel over other systems is its low moisture retentive capacity making the constant flushing of nutrient an essential necessity. With gravel beds, and where power failures are a problem a back-up power system is essential to prevent the beds from drying out.

A word of caution – unless one digs the gravel bed into the earth, don't try and use cables to hold up the plastic sheeting round the edges. They stretch and will not be strong enough to contain the gravel. Only bricks or gum poles will be strong enough to contain a surface-mounted gravel bed.

Sand Beds:

This method of hydroponics is good for growing bulbous or root vegetables such as potatoes, carrots, and turnips..

Sand beds with gum poles (under construction)

Source: DaisyFresh Hydroponics

Care should be taken to use only rough river sand as anything with too fine a particle will clog up the drainage capacity and lead to waterlogging. Unfortunately, much of the sand used in hydroponics has been used up in building and construction, so sand bed constructors must resort to using the smallest size of gravel stone, about 6mm in diameter, which is a good substitute.

To stop leaks from both sand and gravel beds use a 600mm plastic box obtainable from any plastic shop and cut it in half. Then drill a 50mm hole in the bottom and fit a tank fitting to it to which a 50mm drainage pipe can be connected.

Grow-Bag Technique:

This system uses plastic bags to hold the chosen medium. They are usually placed in rows along the floor of a tunnel or growing area in a North to South orientation and the nutrient solution is supplied to the bags by means of LDPE (Low Density Polyethylene) tubing containing micro drippers that feed into the growing medium. The system is relatively cheap to set up but is, of necessity run-to-waste, unless the leachate can be collected in buckets placed underneath the bags to collect and drain it into collection tanks for later

Source: DaisyFresh Hydroponics

re-circulating. The additional cost of the buckets is amortised by the water and fertiliser savings.

Peppers are grown in grow-bags and buckets used to re-circulate the nutrient water. Micro tubing feeds the nutrient water from the top and leachate is collected in the buckets and drains into 50mm white plastic rigid drainage piping and thence into the collection tank.

Two plants can be accommodated in each 12 L bag and 400 bags in an 8m x 30m tunnel or 500 bags in a 10m x 30m tunnel. These numbers convert to 800 and 1000 plants respectively. When fitting out a multispan even denser numbers are possible, depending upon the size of the structure.

Aeroponics

In this system the plants are placed through small holes in a rigid plastic housing structure suspended over micro-jets. The micro-jets supply the nutrient to the roots only and the plants grow suspended above the mist. This system may be more popular overseas than it is in South Africa as the local population is just too small to justify the production of the triangular plant housing required for this method.

Overseas there are instances where Aeroponics is being used with success, notably in some US cities where old disused buildings in the city centres have been converted to aeroponics facilities, combined with LED artificial lighting. Large quantities of salad greens are being produced amidst the very markets that consume them, with a corresponding reduction in transport costs and they can offer employment often where it's most needed.

Cattle fodder can be produced in aeroponic machines which consist of rotating platforms that hold trays of seeds. These chain-driven platforms rotate in a mist of nutrient solution and are housed in a self-contained room. Various sized options are available depending upon the desired output levels.

Deep Water Culture (DWC) – The Floating Raft System

Source: © Banprik | Dreamstime.com

In Japan where dense populations require the production of high volumes of food within a short space of time the construction of waist high reservoirs is undertaken under transparent filtered roof covers. The plants are grown in polystyrene seedling trays that float upon the water which is kept at a constant pH and EC. Large volumes of lettuces for example, can be produced on these expanses of water as the system greatly simplifies the method of nutrient application, sterilisation and light application. Artificial lighting is used to replace the sun's rays at night which can further reduce growing time. The nutrient water is kept correctly oxygenated and at the correct temperature to maximise growth. There are several different systems in operation, based on the same principle. This method can also be used in conjunction with floating fibre mats to produce cattle fodder at high production rates.

Verti-Gro – the World's Finest Vertical Growing System

Home gardeners have used vertical growing for many years; most have limited their experiments to plastic pipes into which holes in the side have been cut. The growing medium is forced into the plastic pipe, which is then erected vertically with or without a facility for collecting the leachate. The main disadvantage of this system is that the medium becomes compressed by the weight of the medium above it, so the further down the column the medium is, the more it is compressed eventually limiting proper drainage. The lower plants die from lack of nutrient and the upper plants do badly from sitting in a too moist an environment. Another system employed a vertical bag culture. The bags (like shoe bags for storing shoes) were hung from tensioned wires strung from the sides of the tunnel with the result that all the weight of the medium, the plants and the nutrient was on the tunnel, which eventually collapsed.

Lettuces and strawberries grown in Verti-Gro

The most successful of all vertical growing systems is a patented one known as **Verti-Gro** that comprises 9 polystyrene 4-litre pots that fit snugly into one another and the column that they form is placed on top of a 10-litre bucket. The medium cannot be compacted as the pots are modular and the ground takes up the weight with no weight on the tunnel structure. Flow through is guaranteed by holes in the pot bases. Through this method six times the number of plants can be fitted into the same area, which brings with it many economic advantages especially where land is in short supply or not suitable for agricultural production.

The following economic advantages are offered by the Verti-Gro system:

• It saves land with more plants per square metre than any other system
• It saves fuel, tractor and labour costs by not having to till and prepare the land for planting.
• It saves fertiliser and lime costs required when planting in open ground
• It saves nutrient and water by re-circulating the nutrient solution
• It saves labour costs by easier, faster picking at comfortable levels
• It saves labour costs by not requiring as much weeding
• It saves capital through re-using the pots over and over
• It saves spraying costs due to lower incidence of pests & diseases
• It saves plastic cover and tunnel costs when using Verti-Gro outdoors
• It increases yield, requiring less fruit culling and greater production of perfect fruit
• Higher yields are obtainable with lower pest and disease infestation

To fully understand the great space saving achievable with Verti-Gro think of the human form. When lying down a human being occupies 6ft x 1ft = 6 square ft, but when standing upright only occupies 1ft x 1ft = 1 square ft. Converted to hectares this means that where a hectare can normally accommodate 50 000 plants, with Verti-Gro it can now accommodate 300 000 plants. This changes the whole breakeven point of an enterprise as less land is needed to grow the same number of plants, or, put another way, more plants can be accommodated in the same extent of land.

The savings in the capital costs of establishment are even greater when one considers the cost of tunnel or multispan structures. Depending on several factors such as the value of the crop being grown, the level of yields and the size of the tunnels, the breakeven point of a hydroponic business will usually be achieved at between 10 and 12 tunnels or between 2800m2 and 3000m2 of growing area. If the same number of plants can be accommodated by the Verti-Gro system in one sixth of the space normally allocated to plants growing horizontally on the ground, it follows that only two tunnels would be required to surpass breakeven instead of 12, a significant saving in the cost of capital investment as represented by both land and buildings.

Source: Verti-Gro Inc. U.S.A

AQUAPONICS

This system of growing plants hydroponically uses fish excrement to supply the nutrients required by plants instead of mixing fertiliser into the water by conventional means. The idea is to save on the cost of nutrients as these would be supplied by the fish and, at the same time, derive an additional income from the sale of the fish once they have grown to maturity. Various fish can be used for the purpose, but Tilapia has proven to be the most popular.

There are a few disadvantages to this method of growing and entry into aquaponics should be considered very carefully before proceeding. Firstly, breeding fish is not without its difficulties and is a science all of its own. It's not just a case of buying the fish and placing them in the water like a goldfish pet at home. Fish can suffer from a variety of maladies and when they do you can't just get the vet in. The first thing you'll know about it probably is when they die. The water has to be kept correctly oxygenated, food must be supplied in the correct amounts, and the water must be at the appropriate temperature, summer and winter, whilst hygiene must be maintained at all times so water sterilisation is also important. Where fish are concerned hygiene is always a moot point, and no cross contamination can be possible into the plant growing area as pathogens would then result in either the death of the plants through phyto-pathological contamination or their pathological contamination which could result in mammalian toxicity such as has occurred with e-coli in organically produced composted tea for use in controlling fungi and other plant diseases.

The other difficulty lies with the proper scientific nutrition of plants. Plants require 16 different nutrients of which gases form three, micro nutrients seven and macro nutrients six. These must all be supplied at a pre-determined ratio depending upon the growth stage of the plant. Fish excrement may supply some of these nutrients, but only in a minority as they could not possibly supply them all, nor in the ratios required by the plant which vary according to the passage of time.

Thus, important micro nutrients like Boron would have to be added, thereby diminishing the utility of procuring the nutrients from the fish. The business of supplying nutrients to plants in the correct ratios is already difficult and complicated – how much more so is it when the ratios supplied by the fish vary and the ratios required by the plants change from time to time?

Aquaponic Food Safety Microbial Threats (Greatest to Least)

1) *Listeria monocytogenes*
2) *Salmonella spp.*
3) *Shiga-toxin E. coli*
4) *Vibrio spp.*
5) *Aeromonas spp.*
6) *Shigella spp.*
7) *Campylobacter spp.*
8) *Pleisomonal shigelloides*
9) *Edwardsiella tarda*
10) *Crypyosporidoum*
11) *Leptospira spp.*

IOWA STATE UNIVERSITY
Extension and Outreach

source: Iowa State University

There are many aquaponic farms over the world, particularly in Japan, but I've not come across convincing results showing significant cost savings by sourcing nitrates from fish excrement. Fish and hydroponic enthusiasts would be better advised to keep the two systems separate.

For these reasons Aquaponics is not a conventional system of hydroponics. Many people have tried aquaponics, and many have had their fingers burnt in the process. It's risky and not to be recommended.

CHAPTER ELEVEN
SYSTEMS – FROM FULLY AUTOMATED TO MANUAL SYSTEMS

One of the beauties of hydroponics is the choice one has between large, fully automated systems to small manual systems. Large scale fully automated hydroponic installations are expensive, but small-scale manually operated systems are equally economical.

The system you decide upon can be tailor-made to your needs and you yourself can design it, provided you keep to within the principles outlined in this book.

A fully automated system requires separate tanks for all the individual nutrients and then mixes them together in pre-weighed amounts according to pre-set parameters, arriving at a tailor made nutritional mix for that plant at that stage of its growth. The size of the nutrient mixing plant will depend upon the size of the hydroponic farm, and how many plants it must feed within a specified period. The interesting part of this type of set-up is that the nutrients are not mixed together to arrive at a certain EC. Rather, they are mixed together by weight relative to a certain amount of water, which then results in an EC outcome, not the other way around. This type of plant alone can cost many thousands of dollars.

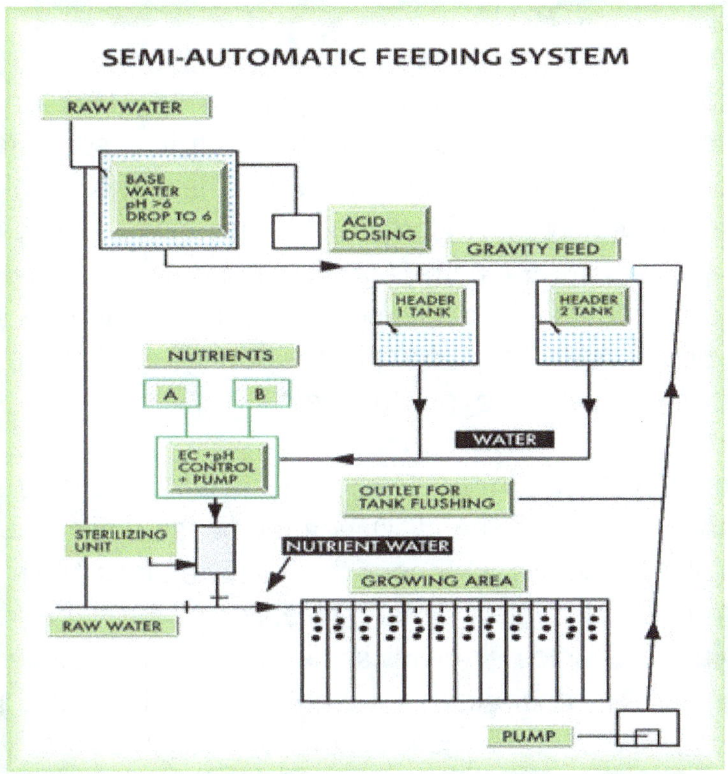

Source: DaisyFresh Hydroponics

The next stage down in automation is a semi-automatic system that can draw in water automatically from source, read and adjust it, feed it to one or more header tanks ready for use, then draw it from the header tank at a pre-determined time, inject the concentrated nutrient feed into the feed line at a rate that will result in a pre-set EC and feed it to a pre-determined area of the farm for a pre-set length of time at a fixed rate of flow, measurable in litres per hour. The nutrient feed is loaded by hand, once every day or two, into nutrient concentration tanks where it is mixed with water ready for injection into the line when called for.

The most economical of these 'fertigation units' when used with an automatic irrigation controller will result in a sophisticated semi-automatic fertigation system where the only human intervention required is to load the nutrient into the concentration tanks and monitor the correct functioning of the system. Feed times and lengths can be pre-set as can the EC and pH levels. This type of system is quite within the bounds of affordability of most commercial hydroponic growers.

A manual system is much cheaper to install, as all the costly automation is done by hand. One of the benefits of automation is reliability, so conversely one of the disadvantages of a manual system is that it relies on the unreliability of the human mind, which in hydroponics is not advisable. If you neglect to feed your plants they will either die or suffer in a way that will affect their growth. There are some controls that one can install to eliminate or partly eliminate these dangers.

A simple manual system can consist of a growing area linked by LDPE 25mm piping to a single tank. There is a given method of working out how many plants can be fed by a 5 000-litre tank and is as follows:

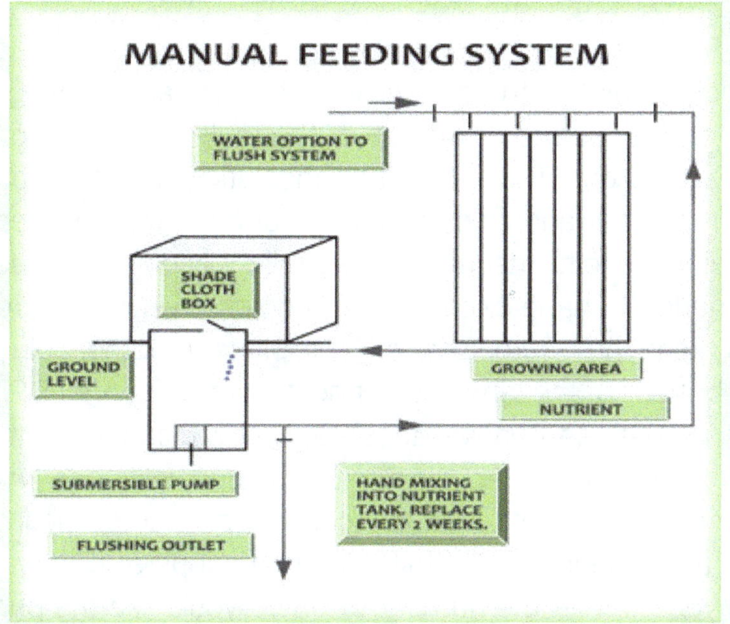

Source: DaisyFresh Hydroponics

Let's assume you have growing bags or growing pots and are using 2-litre/hour drippers. If you feed the plants for half an hour each dripper will require I litre. Therefore, over the period of a half hour your tank can satisfy 5 000 dripper outlets.

From there you can work out how many bags or stacks those drippers will feed. If you've used one dripper per bag then you'll feed 5 000 plants, or two drippers per vertical column will accommodate 2 500 columns. (This is where growing vertically is so economical because 2 500 columns house 2 500 x 36 = 90 000 plants, compared with 5 000 bags on the ground, with only a single dripper per bag per plant, will feed only 5 000 plants). Using this method, you can work out how many or how few 5000 litre tanks you'll require.

By digging holes in the ground for the tanks and burying them (leave about 150mm of the top of the tank protruding to avoid flood waters entering it) you'll be insulating the tanks against heat in summer and cold in winter. Paint the tops of the tanks silver or white to further reflect the sunlight and put a shadecloth box (made of shade cloth and gum poles) over the entire tank area to keep them in the shade. Next, place a submersible pump in the bottom of the tank and connect it to the 25mm LDPE pipe with a T-piece and 2 valves (taps), so that you can dump the nutrient every two weeks by turning the one valve one way and the other valve the other. If you connect an electro-mechanical timer (available in most retail hardware shops at a reasonable price) you can set the number of times you'd like the pump to switch on and for how long. By connecting the leachate drain pipes to the tank and placing the tanks below the growing area you will ensure that the leachate drains back into the tank ready for the next feed. Attach a fresh water tap to the tank so you can fill up when the level drops and connect a discharge outlet pipe to your system so that you can dump the contents every 14 days.

If you combine header tanks below the growing areas with gum poles, shadecloth and a vertical growing system, you'll have a very cost-effective set-up in a very small area relative to the number of plants you could grow.

CHAPTER TWELVE
SYSTEMS – RUN TO WASTE OR RE-CIR-CULATING

In hydroponics, there are two options when it comes to handling leachate. It can be discarded by letting it discharge out of the growing bags, gutters or growing pots and run to waste, draining into the ground or over other crops that may be growing in the vicinity or it can be collected in gutters, drains or pipes and after filtering, fed into a sump or collection tank, into which a sump pump (which will switch on automatically the level reaches a certain point and pump the liquid back to the header tank) is placed.

The first option saves on capital outlay, by avoiding the installation of drainage pipes, tanks and the sump pump, but has the disadvantage of allowing the nutrient-loaded leachate to seep into the water table thus polluting the environment. It also means throwing away costly nutrients. An important factor not to be forgotten when running to waste is that it is essential to allow for 20% of the nutrient solution to run out of the bag or growing containers. This prevents salt (EC) build-up in the bag. Municipal water contains both Sodium and Chlorine, which together form salt (Na Cl). The plant uses chlorine in minute amounts for photosynthesis but doesn't use Sodium at all so causing it to build up in the bag, if not leached out with run-off.

If the leachate is re-circulated economies are achieved, as a complete new batch of nutrient, which would use up the same amount of nutrient and water as the first, does not have to be mixed again and again. Instead, a much lesser amount of nutrient and water would have to be added to the re-circulated leachate to bring it up to the strength required, for use again. This can be done either manually or automatically, depending upon what form of nutrient mixing is being used.

As plants never take up nutrients in precisely the same ratios that they are supplied through the nutrient solution, continuously re-cycling the solutions will lead to an unbalanced nutrient solution in time. Furthermore, sodium that is found in most water supplies combines with chlorine to form salt.
Continuously adding raw water to the nutrient mix to replace transevaporation losses will build up salt to toxic levels at the expense of the balance of the nutrients in the system. To avoid this, *dump the total nutrient solution once every fortnight and start afresh.*

If the decision is made to re-circulate the leachate, take steps to ensure that disease does not enter the system and infect the plants. Several options are available for disease control. The first is hand or manual addition of a disinfectant or sterilising agent such as Sporekill or Teksaclor. This is acceptable but labour intensive, time consuming and reliant on the human memory for fool proof execution. Anything that adds to the overall workload is to be avoided, not because of laziness, but because when all activities are added together on a hydroponic farm, the workload becomes excessive. Therefore, anything that can be undertaken automatically is most desirable.

Ozone gas can be used to eliminate viruses, bacteria and fungi but its use is not recommended. The presence of Ozone gas in the nutrient water is hard to detect and requires constant monitoring, which results in further additions to the workload mentioned earlier. Usually what transpires is that the failure of the Ozone system is first announced by the death of the plants.

A reliable and low-maintenance system for nutrient sterilisation is a UV light sterilisation unit. This will ensure that all the water fed to the plants is free of pathogens, but it will not guarantee that pathogens do not enter the open mouths of the grow bags or pots, so action must be taken to eliminate those as well. The best method of doing this is to ensure that a predatory organism such as Trichoderma (Trichoderma Harzanium) is present in the root zone of the plants before the introduction of the pathogen. To do this the Trichoderma must be mixed into a paste and then introduced into the header tank ready for transmission to the plants at the next feed. During this operation the UV sterilization unit must be switched off, otherwise it will kill off the Trichoderma along with everything else. Don't forget to switch it back on when the introduction of the predatory organism is complete. Keeping the root zones abundant with protective Trichoderma is not cheap, but not nearly as expensive as losing your crop to Phytophthora or Verticillium root rots. You'll need to replenish the Trichoderma about once a month, or more often if you've had a lot of rain. Apply one gram to 4 litres of water.

Just in the same way as advised with the run-to-waste system to flush out the salts by allowing for a 20% run-off, in a re-circulating system you also need to ensure that salts do not build up without restriction. To flush out these salts (Potassium and Magnesium as well as Sodium salts which also give the fertigation meter false EC readings) you MUST dump your entire nutrient feed tank once a fortnight. This can be done by opening the valves on the sump tanks and running the contents to waste, instead of allowing the submersible pump to pump the contents back up to the header tank.

If a salt build-up occurs you will not be alerted to it by changing EC values, as the salts have their own values, which are contributing toward the unchanged EC value. It's merely a change of the balance of the plant food elements that takes place. To eliminate salt build-up in the system, flush out the entire system with water or a very weak nutrient solution.

CHAPTER THIRTEEN
DECIDING WHICH SYSTEMS ARE MOST APPROPRIATE FOR YOU

The choice of the correct system for your requirements largely depends on what types of produce you have decided to grow. Certain vegetables lend themselves more readily to some systems rather than others. The choice is also affected by financial constraints, and the size of the ground available.

As a general guide you may like to use the following groups of plants in the respective system given. The suggestions are somewhat flexible as some plants can grow equally well in more than one system.

Sand or Small Gravel Chips (6mm) in Beds:
Artichoke
Beet
Beetroot
Brussel Sprouts
Carrots
Garlic
Kale
Kohlrabi
Leeks
Marrow
Parsnips
Peas
Potatoes
Rock Melon
Swedes

Sweet potato
Water Cress
Zucchini

Gravel Beds (gravel chips 8 - 10mm)
Beans
Cabbage
Cauliflower
Chicory
Chillies
Fennel
Patty Pan Pumpkins
Pumpkin
Squash
Taro

Nutrient Film Technique (NFT)
Okra
Pak-Choi

Verti-Gro
Broccoli
Celery
Coriander
Endive
Green Onions
Herbs
Horseradish
Lettuce
Mustard
Parsley
Radish
Rhubarb

Salad Greens
Shallot
Silver Beet
Spinach
Spring Onions
Strawberries
Swiss Chard
Tomato

Grow Bags:
Capsicum Peppers
Cucumbers
Egg Plants
Granadillas

Of course, more than one system can be incorporated in a hydroponic farm at the same time and run in parallel with each other.

The relative costs of installing one system versus another should also be considered. Bags are the cheapest, followed by Verti-Gro then NFT and finally, beds, being the most expensive per m2.

There is a method whereby more than one type of vegetable can be cultivated in the same greenhouse together, notwithstanding the fact that different vegetables require different EC levels. This is achieved by grouping the vegetables together so that each group receives the same EC level. They do not have to be grouped together physically but it is more convenient if they are as less tubing is then required.

One or two decimal points variance in EC levels are not critical and experience has found that most vegetables can be grouped together around 1.5EC and 2.4 EC as follows;

Tomatoes, Potatoes, Cabbage etc. = 2.4 EC
The remainder = 1.5 EC

To apply this method to a single growing area, two tanks must be installed with two recirculating systems, both kept separate so that they never intermingle. pH is not a problem either as it can be kept at between 5.5 and 6.0 whatever EC levels are being applied.

The net result is a 'dual parallel recirculating hydroponic fertigation system' which enables the smaller grower to efficiently cultivate several different vegetables in a single area without having to invest in separate multiple greenhouses in order to do so.

When designing your own system start with the basic requirements like a pack house, pump house and storerooms, as these will be essential, and will take up a large part of the budget. You can then expand to the growing areas and add on to them as you grow bigger. It's no good having growing areas if you have nowhere to pack or keep the goods cool.

Keep the buildings reasonably near to the entrance of the ground with the growing areas behind the buildings. Allow for a truck entrance to deliver commodities like pine bark, or fertiliser if you have any open fields as well. Heavy delivery vehicles destroy driveways so there's a need for a separate truck entrance. Allow for a car park for visitors and/or light delivery vehicles.

CHAPTER FOURTEEN
SITE SELECTION, CRITERIA FOR OPTIMUM YIELDS

When selecting a site, you should bear in mind the following:

• The ground should face the opposite slope of the hemisphere in which plants are to be planted. In other words plants destined to grow in the northern hemisphere should face South and vice-versa to optimise light availability.

• If you are going to supply a particular market, then the growing area needs to be as near to that market as practically possible. Petrol/diesel is expensive and vehicle running expenses will be one of the major items featuring on your income and expenditure account, especially when vehicles are used to get your produce to the market daily. If you are, say, 30 km from the market, the return trip is 60kms. Multiply that by 26 delivery days means 1560kms that each truck must drive per month, which will cost a heavy sum per month in fuel per truck. To keep expenses down and be more competitive it's not advisable to site your facility too far from the market.

• Accessibility is also important. It's no good siting your facility on a gravel road that becomes impassable every time it rains. Your clients won't give you extra points for not delivering on rainy days.

• If you orientate your rows from East to West the South or North sides of the plants will not get an even amount of light and you'll end up with uneven growth affected by shade that can affect plant growth.

• The ideal piece of ground should be slightly sloping. 1% to 1.5% is ideal although it's not always possible for nature to comply with our wishes.

• Slope will facilitate natural drainage, whether you are running to waste or re-circulating. Too steep a slope will result in costly earthworks to get the desired platforms on which to site your greenhouse.
• There should be no trees to cast shade on the growing facility. Plants such as strawberries that prefer full sun are adversely affected by shade and can affect the plant growth by as much as 50%.

Check the water quality before you buy. It's no good buying a property with an existing borehole or stream only to find later that the water is unsuitable for hydroponics.

You can have the water analysed by an analytical laboratory or Dept. Agriculture. Be especially wary of properties near the sea as the water table is often brackish and contaminated, mainly by NaCl.

CHAPTER FIFTEEN
CHOOSING THE RIGHT MEDIUM

Source: DaisyFresh Hydroponics

Growing Media:
The variety of media available to the Hydroponic grower is theoretically quite extensive, but in practice boils down to just a few from which to choose. When deciding on a growing medium take the following into account:

• Is it cost-effective?
• Is the quality consistent?
• Is it a renewable resource?
• Are other grower's using it successfully?
• Is it readily available?
• Does it suit my infrastructure and management?

COMPOSTED PINE BARK
Composted pine bark has most of the advantages of other media without their drawbacks. It is readily available (although with deforestation this is becoming a moot point), is relatively stable, takes quite a long time to break down (2-5 years) is inert, and provided it has been composted, does not have the toxins or resins present in some of the other media. Provided your system is sterile, you can re-cycle it, or top up by adding new media. The composting process >50°C kills most pathogens.

You can opt for finely or coarsely screened composted pine bark, depending upon the size and type of what is being grown. Small plants usually require finely screened bark (<6mm). For larger plants and those that require a lot of water like celery one would use coarsely screened composted bark (<15mm). It's also economically priced relative to some of the other media and the pH requires very little adjustment as it's usually around 5.8 to 6.0.

To measure the pH take a mini coffee plunger and fill it with one third media. Then fill with water. Wait 30 minutes before plunging. Pour the water out into a suitable glass or china container and measure the pH. You will be pleasantly surprised.

SAWDUST
Many farmers use pine sawdust medium with great success especially in the grow-bag system. The advantages are that it is easily available and cheap, but the disadvantages are that the nutrient solution tends to tunnel the same way down the bag once it has established a channel, and the suppliers cannot guarantee that it is free of toxins to plants such as resins, tannins or turpentine, depending upon the tree that it comes from or the process to which the timber has been subjected. It also decomposes quicker than pine bark.

WOOD SHAVINGS
Pine bark shavings make a good medium, but the larger particle size does not make it suitable for smaller plants. If, however, you can locate a reliable source of supply, and have the shavings analysed beforehand for phytotoxins, you might find them a very satisfactory medium.

GRAVEL
Gravel is readily available and is the obvious choice in gravel beds, where it doesn't need replenishment like bark. It does, however require some attention; it should be sterilized between each crop and extraneous organic matter, such as old roots and algae needs to be removed. The main disadvantage of gravel is its very low water retention property allowing no margin of error with the watering programme. It's also heavy to handle and is the

costliest of all the systems to set up, as additional components are also required to complete the bed. Pink gravel has a pH of 5.8 while grey gravel's pH is about 6.1.

COIR COCO PEAT OR COCOS
This medium has increased in popularity over the years with seedling growers in particular who often mix it with pine bark when growing smaller plants such as seedlings. However, in some systems it needs careful monitoring if it is to be used successfully. In a vertical system where drainage is of paramount importance, it can retard the drainage capacity of the column thus preventing nutrient from getting to the lower reaches of the stack. This slow drainage can also result in the plants suffering from lack of Oxygen. Coir's high water-retention factor can result in a water-logged medium. Plants require a moist medium, neither too wet nor too dry. A good description of the perfect moisture content for a plant is that of 'a freshly squeezed sponge'.

Some coir imports have also been suspect as they've contained too much salt (NaCl). Most coir comes from palm trees in Sri Lanka and it's clear that it hadn't been properly washed and cleaned of sea salt before shipment. Be wary of coir. It's not a medium to be used with abandon and requires careful management.

The recent exports of Mozambican coir have a low EC and thus look promising. The EC should be below 1.5 micro Siemens before adding fertiliser.

POLYSTYRENE

This material is sometimes used as a constituent of media to increase drainage. With manufacture linked to the oil price it's not that cheap and being non-biodegradable, creates disposal problems.

ROCKWOOL

Rockwool is made from igneous rock heated to very high temperatures whose fibres are spun off to create a medium suitable for hydroponics. It's expensive and not readily available although widely used elsewhere in some countries such as Australia.

PERLITE

This is a volcanic glass in the form of granules (like mineral foam). There are certain advantages in using Perlite. It is stable and doesn't break down and maintains a constant pH. It is locally available. It doesn't need constant replenishment so can be considered an energy saving resource. Flower growing has employed perlite with very successful results. If your budget can afford perlite it would be wise to invest in it although the initial cost might be quite high. The advantage of having a neutral pH cannot be overemphasised.

VERMICULITE

This has a high water holding capacity, but the cellular structure breaks down easily. It goes pasty after a while. It's readily available but the relatively high pH (7 - 9) is a disadvantage in hydroponic systems unless compensating adjustments are made. This is another unnecessary activity where one is looking for labour saving devices and fewer activities.

SAND

Sand has much the same characteristics as gravel above, except that the particles are smaller. It's a very useful medium for growing root or bulbous vegetables. A distinction must be made between coarse sand suitable for hydroponics and fine sand which is not suitable due to its inability to drain easily. Use coarse river sand if you can obtain it. Unfortunately, the building industry competes with hydroponics for the consumption of sand, so it is becoming increasingly more difficult to obtain supplies of good quality coarse sand. If it's difficult to obtain, a good substitute is fine gravel < 6mm.

LECA (LIGHT EXPANDED CLAY AGGREGATE)

Technically, this medium has all the advantages of Perlite. The pH is stable and neutral and it is made from kiln dried clay and it doesn't break down. The particles are a mixture of small, medium and large balls which are ideal for root stability, and high air-filled porosity. However, the high price of this medium is a disadvantage if used commercially.

PEAT

Used widely in Europe sphagnum peat is not available universally and being an exhaustible resource is not ecologically desirable.

CLINKER

Cheap, but generally only used as a filler with other media.

COCONUT HUSKS
These are a good medium with much the same characteristics as wood shavings. If they are readily available at an economical cost, they make a good choice.

The choice of the correct growing medium will depend on economics, availability as well as the plant's requirements for moisture or good drainage. Watering schedules must be adjusted according to the different media employed.

An indication of a medium's water holding capacity or its ability to drain well is to measure its AFP (air filled porosity). AFP is a measurement of the air surrounding the particles that comprise the medium. To measure AFP, take a small glass and fill it with the medium. Then slowly top up with water until it reaches the brim. Then hold the medium in the glass with one hand while pouring out the water into a second identical glass. The amount of water collected in the second glass represents the % AFP.

• AFP > 35% the medium is very open, it drains quickly and requires very regular watering, at least daily such as coarse river sand, perlite, LECA and gravel.
• AFP 15% - 35% drains well, requires reasonable watering, such as screened composted pine bark.
• AFP < 15%, prone to waterlogging, such as fine sand, and coco peat.
• As AFP increases, watering frequency must be shortened to avoid drying out.
• As AFP decreases, watering frequency must be extended to avoid waterlogging and oxygen deprivation.

CHAPTER SIXTEEN
TUNNEL COVERINGS - WHICH IS BEST FOR THE CLIMATE?

PLASTIC OR SHADECLOTH:

In the 17th Century when glass had been invented in Europe farmers made glasshouses in which they could grow fruits and vegetables that otherwise couldn't be grown because of the cold climate. The glass had two functions. It kept the cold air out, protected the plants from the wind and snow, and allowed the sun's rays to penetrate and so heated the inside of the greenhouse. To this day large numbers of tomatoes are grown in green houses in places like Guernsey, where it would otherwise be too cold to do so successfully.

In Europe they do not have to worry about hail, but glass greenhouses are impractical in hail prevalent countries. With the arrival of plastics, it became possible to build plastic covered tunnels to prevent inclement weather from damaging the plants. However, plastic is not without problems that the manufacturers and vendors will be sure not to tell you about.

Firstly plastic, whilst efficiently keeping out wind and rain, allows the sun's rays to penetrate during the day causing the inside of the tunnel to become excessively hot, with temperatures soaring as high as 55 deg. C. This can be effectively countered by cooling the tunnel with a pad and fan system, which is costly to buy and run, requiring electricity and water to function effectively.

Over and above that it interferes with the humidity levels, which can be beneficial in areas with inherently low relative humidity (Rh) such as in high cool areas, but negative in high humidity areas such as in coastal low-lying areas. Cooling systems such as humidifiers or misters that rely on water for cooling interfere with the humidity levels in the tunnels.

What is the point of installing plastic covered tunnels at great expense? The object of the glass greenhouses in Europe was to increase the ambient temperatures in a cold climate, not to heat up the inside of the tunnel in an inherently warm climate. Plastic is useful where the climate is cold such as in winter and the winter sun's rays are able to radiate through the plastic and heat up the inside of the tunnel. Growers must however remember that in cold places night times can be very cold which plastic covering does very little to change. It merely keeps the wind out and prevents the wind chill factor from lowering the temperature further. Growers, who want to create an artificially warm climate to grow produce like peppers for example, would still have to heat the tunnels at night using some form of artificial heating such as a boiler, steam and hot water pipes.

As far as the coastal areas are concerned plastic is not to be recommended *unless the structures are well ventilated.* Shade cloth structures are often more suitable. Where the grower is dealing with a crop such as peppers that require heating at night in winter, this can be done with a boiler and piped hot water. The pipes are run on the floor under the plants and heat the plants before the heat rises and escapes into the atmosphere.

The fact that it later escapes is of no consequence as it will already have completed its job of supplying growing heat to the plants. The problem then arises as to how the growing houses are to be cooled during the day.

Shade cloth is relatively cheap, easily available, and comes in varying occluding percentages to cater for the different crops that prefer more or less shade. Shadecloth is designated by is ability to occlude ultra violet rays and not light, so be careful when specifying which % you require. For example, a 40% white shadecloth keeps 40% of the UV light out but only offers about 15% of complete shade to the plants. With black on the other hand, the % shade designation is identical for total shade and UV light, so there is no confusion there.

Other colours offer differing percentages; rather consult the following table before deciding:

Shade Cloth Code	Colour	Shade Factor %	UV Block %
20	Black	20	20
20	White	8	20
30	Black	30	30
30	White	12	30
40	Black	40	40
40	White	15	40
40	Green	37	40
50	Black	50	50
50	White	16	50
50	Green	42	50
60	Black	60	60
60	White	16	60
70	Black	70	70
80	Black	80	80
80	White	32	80
80	Green	76	80
90	Black	90	90

Seedling Growers have been using shade cloth and gum poles for their structures for many years and are still doing so.

Because of high humidity levels, especially in summer, plastic and steel structures are not recommended within at least 60km of the coastline, depending on the altitude. In Kenya, strawberries are grown on the slopes of Mount Kenya, despite being on the Equator, simply because of the cold environment caused by the high altitude.

A shade cloth structure 'breathes', which reduces humidity as the structure is ventilated and thus lowers the incidence of fungal diseases.

TUNNELS OR WOODEN POLES:
The decision to erect costly metal tunnels or to opt for much cheaper treated wooden poles largely depends on the decision whether or not to use plastic or shade cloth. If the decision is to use plastic because of a generally colder climate and benefit from the sun's radiation during the day time then the purchase and erection of galvanised tunnels will be a foregone conclusion, as it is not advisable to use wooden poles as supports for plastic because of the high risk of damage to the plastic.

When opting for steel tunnels do not try and skimp on essential factors such as the galvanising. Un-galvanised steel will rust in no time. You will also need to use 50mm steel tubing for the outer piping and concrete them into the ground.

This will ensure that they with stand wind velocities of over 100 k.p.h. and that you don't end up with 'spaghetti' after a fierce storm. Farmers have been driven out of business through not having tubing of sufficient strength to withstand rogue winds that hit some coastal areas from time to time.

Shade cloth is the cheaper option, and where climatic conditions favour its use wooden pole structures can further economise the capital cost of establishment. CCA (Chromium, Copper and Arsenic) treated poles (3,6m x 80 to 100mm) are relatively inexpensive if purchased direct from supplier. Thus, an enclosure of 20m x 20m or 400m2 with poles every 2.85m apart, using dual support lines in the centre that would require 40 poles would cost about a third less than a steel structure. Reinforcing duckbill anchors also need to be used to brace the outside poles against high winds, which will add to the cost. However, an alternative to duck bill anchors is to dig a trench one metre deep and place old tyres in it. The poles can then be attached to the tyre with wire or steel cables equipped with tensioners (knuckles) and the trench filled in.

It would certainly pay you to investigate the cost of erecting gum poles and shadecloth in combination with Verti-Gro columns (for maximum plant density), fertigation tubing and re-circulating plumbing. At a rough estimate the costs of wooden poles and shadecloth are 50% cheaper than metal and .

MULTISPANS:

Source: DaisyFresh Hydroponics

A multispan is a single large structure that can be tailor-built to the grower's specification. Provided the ground does not slope too steeply (not more than about 2%) a single large structure eliminates the need for individual tunnel sides and incorporates the entire growing area under a single roof. It also offers cost-savings by having one centralised climate control for the entire multispan instead of having individually climate-controlled greenhouses.

Sometimes, depending upon the topography, it's just not possible to build a multispan, and individual platforms must be levelled in order to accommodate the greenhouses. However, if uneven or too steep ground is not a problem and multispans can be accommodated significant savings can be made. Ten greenhouses, each covering 300m2 could be alternatively accommodated by a single multispan of 3000m2.

An additional advantage presented by a multispan is the fact that they are normally quite high structures (4-5m) and ventilation is incorporated into the sides and/or roof allowing the concomitant reduction in humidity and temperature, so important in areas where these two factors would make growing crops difficult.

CHAPTER SEVENTEEN
BUILDINGS - PACK HOUSES, PUMP HOUSES, CHEMICAL STORES

To save money on buildings, use the modern system of polystyrene lined with Chromadek, (powder coated aluminium) for your construction. It's very aesthetic and costs about a quarter of the price of bricks and mortar. Details are available under the suppliers' lists at the back of this book.

The pack house is one of the critical areas examined very closely by GLOBAL GAP, so if you intend becoming accredited at a later stage, do make sure that the buildings conform to the GLOBAL GAP protocols before you start so that you are not involved in costly alterations later. Basically, the packing area should be kept sacrosanct and toilets, lunch rooms, change rooms, chemical or other stores must not open on to the packing area. A manager or supervisor's office, a chiller and packaging materials storeroom are where direct access is permitted. All other rooms must have separate entrances accessible from the outside only.

When building, take into account the following:
o The pack house should be well insulated to keep produce cool
o Whirlybirds in the roof remove the hot air from the space under the roof
o The pack room will need air conditioning as well as a chiller
o Build it bigger than initially required to allow for growth

o Build a separate storeroom for poisons and chemical sprays away from the pack house. If it's to be in the same building it must have a separate entrance.

When building a pump house do it with bricks and mortar, or polystyrene and Chromadek panels, and make sure that it is big enough to accommodate extra equipment as you grow. The minimum size recommended is 3 x 4 metres, to ensure access to and around equipment when it requires attention. Keep nutrients separate from other storage items such as packaging. Keep all storage items on plastic pallets so that they're off the floor and won't be damaged by potential spillage. Keep liquids below powders.

CHAPTER EIGHTEEN
PESTS AND DISEASES - GOOD MANAGEMENT; BIOLOGICAL CONTROLS

Once you've set up your hydroponicum and the feeding system is operating without a problem, the plants are growing nicely, and you think you're on the way to reaping a good crop that'll bring you in some nice cash, be warned, you might be in for a nasty surprise. When you least expect it you'll suddenly find that something is attacking your plants or that they become sickly for no apparent reason. This is a depressing situation not only for the plants but more seriously, for you and your pocket.

You can minimise the chance of this happening. Firstly, ensure that you have a full understanding of nutrition in the preceding section. A healthy plant is much more able to resist attacks by pests and diseases than a sickly one. It seems to be part of nature's elimination process, or natural selection. If your plants are not looking healthy because of some symptom, first make sure that it's not a nutritional problem, toxicity or deficiency. Check water flow and drainage to make sure they are receiving enough water. Are the symptoms widespread or limited to one or two plants here and there? Check reference manuals and find out whether the symptom is caused by a pest (the plants are usually eaten in a local spot) or a disease (the symptoms are usually more widespread affecting the whole plant).

As bacteria, virus or fungus can cause diseases, it's important to know which one of these has caused the problem and counteract it to achieve control.

Pests and diseases are so costly, not only because of the damage they cause to the crop but because of the cost of substances used to eradicate them, that their symptoms can cause apoplexy in even the most serene of farmers. So much so that a recognised system has now been developed to deal with them even before they arise. It's called INTEGRATED PEST MANAGEMENT and it's a co-ordinated and effective programme that seeks to prevent the ingress of pests and diseases before they occur, then to monitor the incidence or level of pests and diseases so that the farmer can be alerted when safe levels are exceeded, and finally to take effective action to eliminate the threat permanently without damage to the crop or danger to human life. It's in your best interests to learn whatever you can about IPM and take your own action to implement it. Here are some suggestions:

Because pests and diseases thrive in a closed environment (once pests get in they have no predators) it's essential that you monitor them by erecting sticky traps in strategic places around the growing area. These traps are designed to alert you to the population of the pest and not only to reduce it, which of course it does marginally.

Introduce a daily scouting programme to nip any pests or disease in the bud - a stitch in time saves nine. Don't forget to look on the underside of the leaves, as you'll seldom find the insects on the top.

Refer below for an example of a form the plant carers can use to fill in and give you whenever they come across a problem.

Plant Health Report

WHERE APPLICABLE, THIS REPORT MUST BE COMPLETED BY THE SUPERVISOR BEFORE 9AM

DATE: _______ day, _________ stth of _____________ 20___   Tunnel Number | _______

Temperatures Maximum _________ Minimum _________ Present _________ Time _________

#						ALERT BOARD
1.	BASIC STRUCTURE	BREACHED	BENT	DAMAGED	INTACT	
2.	COVERING	TORN	DAMAGED	DIRTY	INTACT	
3.	GROWING POTS	UPRIGHT	DAMAGED	WHERE	INTACT	
4.	FLOOR COVERING	TORN/WORN	WATER	WHERE	INTACT	
5.	PLANTS	DISEASE	PESTS	WHERE	INTACT	
6.	IRRIGATION TUBING	LEAKING	OTHER	WHERE	INTACT	
7.	DRAINAGE TUBING	LEAKING	OTHER	WHERE	INTACT	
8.	EMITTERS	BLOCKED	FIXED	WHERE		
9.	COOLING SYSTEM	FAN WORKING	WET WALL - ALGAE PRESENT	OK		

10. OTHER COMMENTS _______________________________________

____

____

____

NAME: _________________ SIGNED: _________________

Plant Health Report.doc/08/03/2017

85

When using chemical remedies make sure thatworkers are properly equipped and dressed in goggles, gloves and spray overalls. They should be trained in the proper way of handling chemicals, particularly with mixing and dosages. Too high a concentration can damage the plants and too low will not be effective. The containers of toxic chemicals are labelled according to the degree of toxicity and are as follows:

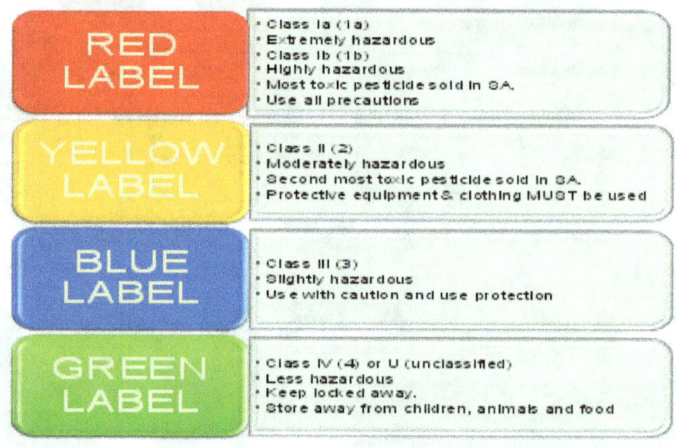

Source: DaisyFresh Hydroponics

Make sure that the growing environment is free of weeds which often act as hosts for insects and disease. All dead organic matter must be removed from the growing area immediately and not left on the ground to rot.

Once you've identified what's damaging your plants, counteract it with the correct spray. Try to apply organic or natural countermeasures first as they are safer to use and will have fewer potential repercussions for the eating public. When using a toxic chemical follow the dosage directions closely, and follow the equipment washing instructions even more closely.

If it's toxic it'll probably have a withholding period, so make sure you adhere to it - if you don't it could be lethal - See GLOBAL GAP below. To be effective it's essential to acquire a motorised backpack sprayer. This is because the sprayer must be able to get to the underside of the leaves and inside the growing whorls where the insects hide. Hand sprayers do not have the power to do that. Remember to spray up to the point of run-off, no more.

Spraying cannot take place in adverse climatic conditions. Too high winds > 8kph will result in spray drift, rain will dilute it and excess heat will burn the plants. Spray only in optimal conditions.

Many spray chemicals require the use of wetters, although recently one or two have made their appearance that don't. Check label instructions carefully. A chemical that requires a wetter/spreader is ineffectual without it!

It's a good idea, as part of the IPM, to draw up a list of the pests and diseases that you come across, and alongside that heading enter the chemical or organic substance you used together with its efficacy. This will help later when you again come across the same pest or disease. By then you probably won't remember which countermeasure you used, never mind which one was most effective. There are so many spray remedies that you'll have to start again and go through the whole time-consuming process, unless you have that information readily to hand. Training the workers is also very important and a part of GLOBAL GAP.

BIOLOGICAL CONTROLS

In the past the use of toxic chemicals was widely used to control pests and diseases. However, this led to some unsatisfactory outcomes. Starting with DDT in the 60's, which was used (and still is in some places) to control the female Mephistopheles mosquito from spreading malaria, toxic chemicals can produce undesirable effects in humans. DDT for example, builds up in the human body; it accumulates in the liver and kidneys which are not able to metabolise the poison, resulting eventually in disease and death.

Other equally undesirable side-effects can be produced by the toxicity of various chemicals so their control is monitored by Agricultural Act 36 of 1947 and only registered chemicals should be applied to specific crops. Furthermore, withholding periods should be adhered to, to allow the chemical residue to dissipate sufficiently to enable human consumption without any deleterious effects. In practice this just doesn't work. Manufacturers don't register many of their products because of the expense involved and farmers are forced to use unregistered chemicals to achieve control. In addition, time pressure on farmers to produce their crops quickly or harvest them before they become overripe, means that often they are not able to adhere to the specified withholding periods. In any event, there can be no control over either of these two circumstances which is not satisfactory.

Biological science has now discovered that there are a number of naturally occurring bio organisms that are highly effective in controlling certain pests and diseases, and these are becoming increasingly available commercially by companies who harvest, breed and store them ready for agricultural applications. The consumer pressure to produce fresh produce organically no doubt put pressure on manufacturers to find a more practical and satisfactory solution to pest and disease control. Bio organisms that achieve this end are being discovered and used more widely and currently the following are available for the listed plant pathological maladies:

Trichoderma Harzanium (commonly known as Trichoderma; trade name "Eco T"). Widely used as a drench or nutrient solution additive to control root rots such as Verticillium and Phytopthera it also controls Botrytis, Powdery Mildew, Anthracnose and other fungal diseases.

Beauvaria Bassiana (commonly referred to as BB Plus) controls aphids and red spider mites

Bacillus Thurengensis (trade name Dipel DF) used against Lepidoptera (caterpillar worm larvae)

Biological tea; used as a broad-spectrum fungicide for the control of fungal infections in roots and leaves. It can be applied as a spray or through the dripper system. This is not to be confused with composted tea which is not recommended as this can contain an uncontrolled number of bio-organisms including pathological ones such as e-coli. Biological tea is the result of a clinically controlled process, containing predatory organisms for the control of plant diseases and fungi and indicated for application on plants destined for human consumption.

Citric Acid and Borax: Known as WETCIT (previously was PREV-AM) is an easy to use, pleasant smelling and effective remedy for use against an unusual combination of powdery mildew and red spider mite.

The advantages of these biological remedies are that they are non-toxic to humans and can be used without any withholding periods. There is no resistance build up by the pests as with chemical remedies. They can also be used as a preventative measure and introduced or sprayed before any signs of the pest or disease have manifested, which is highly efficient and effective.

This is not an exhaustive list and many more are available for specialised applications. Others are fast being identified and marketed so constant reference should be made to suppliers for new information on this exciting new range of pesticides and fungicides.

To help you identify some of the pests you may come across some colour photos are reproduced on the following pages.

Pest Library

Source: Do-Your-Own-Pest-Control.Com

Source: Do-Your-Own-Pest-Control.Com

Source: Do-Your-Own-Pest-Control.Com

Here are some of the more common pests and diseases that you'll be likely to come across with some suggested remedies:

Pests	Chemical	Biological/Organic
American Bollworm	Deltamethrin	Beauvaria Bassiana
Ants	Deltamethrin	Sugar, Flour, Borax
Aphis	Demiton	Beauvaria Bassiana
Cabbage worm	Methomex	Beauvaria Bassiana
Caterpillars	Deltamethrin	Bacillus Thurengensis
Cutworms	Deltamethrin	Bacillus Thurengensis
Diamond Back Moth	Methomex	Beauvaria Bassiana
Fruit Fly	Spinosad	Vegol
Leaf Hoppers	Abamectin	Prevam/Wetcit
Leaf Miners	Abamectin	Prevam/Wetcit
Loopers	Methomex	Beauvaria Bassiana
Mealybugs	Chlorpyrifos	Vegol
Nematodes	Ethoprophos	Trico Asperellum
Rats and Mice	Storm	Traps
Red Spider Mite	Abamectin	Beauvaria Bassiana
Snails, slugs	Snail Bait	Beer*
Thrips	Methomex	Vegol
Whitefly	Mosipilan	PrevAm

*Place beer in a shallow tray - they drown in it

Diseases	Chemical	Biological/Organic
Anthracnose	Copper Oxy Cl	Trichoderma var 77
Blossom End Rot	Ditto	Ditto
Bacterial Spot	Ditto	Ditto
Botrytis	Ditto	Ditto
Damping Off	Ditto	Ditto
Powdery Mildew	Copper Oxy Cl, Sulf.	Bacillus Subtilus
Root Rots : Fusarium, Verticillium, Phytopthera	Metalaxyl,	Bio Sulphur Bio Silica

CHAPTER NINETEEN
ORGANICS - HOW TO BE
ORGANIC-HYDROPONIC

The introduction of organics into farming methods, spearheaded by trends in Europe and America, is also being evidenced in some other countries, but the impact there, for various reasons, is considerably muted, compared with countries where the standard of living is higher. You may have seen that many shops are offering organically grown meats, fruits and vegetables now. Some of these are cleverly packaged to disguise the fact that they are priced considerably more than normal produce.

Cultivation of fresh produce organically requires the preparation of soils following organic methods which prescribe the use of compost and no artificial fertilisers. Also, control of pests and diseases must follow organic protocols which prohibit the use of chemical pesticides. Fields cannot be used to plant the same crops or family of crops year after year and must also be left fallow for a season every few years.

As far as hydroponics is concerned, the molecules of the minerals used in nutrition are identical whether produced from compost or in a chemical factory, and now with the advent of biologicals, these can be used in pest and disease control whether the plants are grown organically or hydroponically.

However to be certified as 'organic hydroponic' you will most certainly have to produce the nitrates and phosphate fertilisers using bio-organisms to do this. BioTecnica supply a bio brewer and the bio-organisms that do this under the brand name 'Bactolife AF.' Most reasonable accreditation bodies will accept your being 'organic-hydroponic' if you produce the phosphates and nitrates in this way, but accreditation is not guaranteed as each body is a law unto themselves. If you have open ground and are growing by drip irrigation in addition to hydroponics, you can apply chicken litter for example, instead of fertiliser.

Organic accreditation is extremely haphazard and there is no international body that sets standards for organics. The net result is that standards vary from country to country and in the USA some states supply unaccredited organic produce to other states where it is accredited.

No one knows whether organics will continue or for how long. In Europe where the standard of living is higher, a minimum % of the population might keep it alive for longer, but in many countries, especially African ones, where many are living below the bread line, it cannot make a significant impact. If the world must learn to feed itself it must increase the productivity of food production in line with the population increase, and it won't be able to do that with organics.

CHAPTER TWENTY
MARKETING - DO YOUR HOMEWORK

Many farmers, especially hydroponic or horticultural farmers, seem to know nothing or very little about marketing when they first start out. They then learn the hard way.

The hard way is exemplified by a woman who started out with great enthusiasm and grew a crop of lettuces. They took about five weeks to mature, which is about normal, and with her beginner's luck the quality was just about perfect.

When they were ready for cutting, she approached her preferred retailer with the news that she had a boat load of lettuces of the best quality for them and expected to be received with great enthusiasm and offered the highest price. To her dismay, they regarded the event somewhat diffidently and replied saying that they had no need for further lettuces as they already had three suppliers who were giving them the good quality they required. Her dismay turned to panic after she visited two other retailers each of whom reacted similarly. Crestfallen and disappointed, she returned to her farm, now desperate to find an outlet so as not to lose money. She sent off a truck loaded with lettuces and it went from small shop to small shop where it managed to sell off 5 to 10 lettuces a time, but all at a reduced price. The truck returned at the end of the day with only half its load sold, which barely covered the diesel.

The next day she resolved to take a load to the municipal market in the hope of being able to sell more than she 'd been able to do so far. The agent took them, so the next day she phoned him up to find out how much he'd got for them." Oh, I sold a few at 0.15c a head "he said, "but most of them are still here as there's a glut of them at the moment. Phone me up next week and we can see whether things are any better." So, the next week she phoned him eager to dispose of her crop which was now past optimal picking point. "Oh", he said, "you can send a few, but no more than last week". Her situation was desperate as 90% of the lettuces were still in the ground. Over the next week she sold another 10% of the crop until they all began to bolt and turn yellow with age. She lost 80% of her crop and the 20% she sold was disposed of at a giveaway price because supply outstripped demand at that point in the growing season. The whole exercise was a complete loss as she wasn't even able to recuperate the costs of nutrients, labour, seedlings or diesel. What is the lesson to be learned here? Do your homework. Find out beforehand whether the retailer can take a specific crop at a particular time. There is a glut of lettuces during winter as they are easy to grow then. Conversely, if you have cool tunnels and can grow them in January and February without them bolting you can command a good price. Find out what is in short supply and when. Use the market statistics to help you.

Never plant your entire crop in a single fruit or vegetable. Spread your risk. Plant a little of each type over different periods of the year. That will keep your turnover even.

Stagger your plantings so that they ripen over a long period of time and not all at once. If you deliver large quantities to the Municipal markets you'll crash the price and get very little for your hard work.

The objective in good marketing is to ensure that you have an outlet for your produce when it ripens. Marketing is defined as "creating the right environment in which the sale can take place".

Advertising forms a large part of marketing, but it's not viable for a small farmer to advertise anywhere in the press, radio or television. Therefore, advertising must be undertaken by the farmer himself or a sales rep if he is big enough. Nothing can beat the personal touch, and customers are impressed by a farmer touting freshly grown produce. It reassures them that they'll get personal attention and farm-fresh produce. Even if you don't manage to get in with a retailer you can visit shops, restaurants and wholesalers. This needs to be done in two stages. The first stage is before you decide which crops to plant and the second is when you've picked the first ripe samples that you can take on a follow-up visit to the customers to entrench the deals.

Nothing beats personal attention and you have to leave the farm on a couple of mornings a month to keep in contact. If you neglect your customers they'll eventually leave you. If you have a friendly, outward going personality this will work in your favour as these personality types tend to make the best salesmen or women.

Making the sale:
There are three aspects to a sale that need to be satisfied if one
is to be successful. The customer needs to be convinced of your
quality, happy with your price and believe in your reliability. So, in
a nutshell it's all about PRICE, QUALITY AND SERVICE. If one of
these is absent or not up to par you'll either not get, or you'll lose,
the sale. Before you try and sell him your product find out from
him what he's paying, how reliable is the quality and how good is
the service. Does he ever have stock-outs? Is the quality
consistent? He must be convinced that he's going to be better
off by buying from you than his present supplier. Don't be afraid
to ask questions to establish the current situation. People enjoy
talking about themselves and their business.

In order for you to keep abreast of the market price it's a good
idea to use FNB market statistics on the internet. It costs about
US$250 per month but that way you'll know what is the going
price, so you can alter your price accordingly in line with it. If your
price is too high when others go down you could lose the
business, and if your price is too low you'll not be maximising
your profits.
You can call on the Government hospitals and school feeding
schemes and tender for their business. These can be massive,
so once you've been awarded the tender make sure you don't
lose it again as is you do it could leave a huge hole in your
turnover. The same goes for a retailer. The optimal situation for
you is when production and sales are consistently at the same
level. Production should mirror sales and vice versa.

CHAPTER TWENTY-ONE
HYGIENE AND PACKAGING

Whether you supply a retail supermarket or private customers make sure that your presentation attracts customers making them want to buy your product. If you had to choose between a crisp green lettuce in a cellophane bag or a drooping, matt, fading one just lying on the bottom of a cardboard box, which would you choose?

Modern packaging has become an essential part of marketing, despite what all the green people say, so make sure that you have the right packaging for the right produce. Sometimes this can be a battle to establish, but the list of suppliers at the back of this book under the Reference Section, should help you.

The Supermarket retailers will standardise on their packaging for all their products and will inform you where supplies may be obtained. You pay for the sleeves, labels and bar codes as well as the sell-by best-by stickers and you then recover these costs in the selling price. The costs of hiring lugs must also be factored in.

Your packers must be trained to wash their hands between every nose wipe, after they've been to the toilet and had something to eat. If they have a cold they should be sent home, as a packer with a cold just cannot work hygienically. Use Bob caps to stop hair falling on the food and overalls or dust coats are obligatory to stop personal

unwashed clothes from coming into contact with the food.
No jewellery or earrings, no skin bracelets allowed.
All these things might seem trivial, but they will save your bacon
and reputation in the long haul. If an earring is found in a
lettuce your reputation suffers and so does that of the outlet. If it
happens to a supermarket retailer there's a huge outcry together
with an investigation. Because the competition between
retailers is so great they replace the merchandise free of charge,
so it costs them and they re-act correspondingly harshly. You do
NOT want to experience this.

CHAPTER TWENTY-TWO
TRANSPORTATION

You'll need to transport the produce to your customers, and to do it properly you'll require a refrigerated truck. Without one you'll run the risk of the produce arriving limp and tired in summer (especially spinach and lettuce), shelf life will be reduced and come-backs will escalate. Supermarket retailers will not allow you to deliver in anything else. A one and half ton refrigerated truck will do the job admirably and you can save yourself money by getting a second hand one up to two years old.

New vehicles drop in value by 25% once they've been driven off the showroom floor so a good way to save money in to get a low mileage used vehicle. You can have the old load box removed and add a refrigerated box to it but don't skimp with the refrigeration. If you do you'll curse your decision every time it breaks down and you have to take the truck off the road for a few days to have it repaired. A reliable refrigeration unit is almost as important as a reliable vehicle because the two are linked together and when the fridge breaks down you can't just unbolt it and send it in for service. The whole vehicle is affected. Once a few years have passed and it's time to upgrade you can take the refrigerated box and refrigerating unit off, buy a second-hand load bin for the old truck and sell it off at a reasonable price which will off-set the cost of the new vehicle for which you now will not have to buy a new box and fridge. This is another good way to keep costs down.

If you keep the trucks clean and in good condition they'll create a much better impression than if they are dirty. You would think twice about moving your furniture in a damaged furniture removal van. If you insist on a weekly wash outside and inside, and keep them serviced, it'll save you in the long run.

Keep logs. You are obliged to do so anyway if you conform to Global Gap.

CHAPTER TWENTY-THREE
GLOBAL GAP - HYGIENIC STANDARDS FOR THE FOOD INDUSTRY

Supermarket retailers insist on conformance to Global Gap standards.

Global Gap is an international body, based in Bonn, Germany, that has set hygienic and safety standards for the food industry. The protocols are onerous and the audit expensive, as well as being yet another expense in a long list of them that beset anyone in the food growing and supplying industry.

Among other things they require that you train your staff in every area and every activity in which they are involved. You will have to clothe them properly while at work. You will be required to store chemicals and nutrients separately and in a special way. You will be required to keep logs of all activities and in particular you will have to be able to maintain traceability of your produce to the point of origin. Minimum safety standards are required for the pack houses and growing areas, vehicles must be washed and serviced regularly, and you'll have to produce logs or evidence that this has been done. All equipment such as scales must be serviced regularly, and proof must be supplied.

Nothing can be sprayed on to plants that is not registered under the relevant Agricultural Act and this includes non-toxic biological substances so be very careful what you apply and read the labels.

If you're spraying peppers for example, it's no good using the chemicals that are registered for tomatoes just because they are similar, and think you'll get away with it. If the chemicals are not registered specifically for peppers you'll fail the GLOBAL GAP audit. This can be extremely irritating and not logical. If you fail the audit because of non-adherence to this particular protocol you'll find that some retailers are more understanding than others about it. If you can supply evidence that a particular chemical is used on your crop in USA or Europe most auditors will accept it.

Most chemicals have a stated withholding period during which the fruit or plant cannot be used for human consumption. This allows the toxic element in the chemical to dissipate through natural processes and renders the plant harmless for human consumption. You'll have to log adherence to these withholding periods specified by manufacturers.

Protocols are divided into Major Musts where you are obliged to conform fully to all these; a single failure and you fail the audit and Minor Musts where you can fail one or two of these without failing the audit, but are strongly recommended to correct the failure, which in any event must be corrected by the time you have the subsequent audit. The remainder of the protocols are 'recommended' and you are required to achieve a minimum percentage to pass. Every successive year should be an improvement on past years.

One of the most important aspects of GLOBAL GAP affects the layout of the buildings and pack room, so it's a good idea to find out who the GLOBAL GAP auditor is before you build and get a copy of the protocols from him. If your buildings conform to the protocols then you won't be involved in costly alterations later. This is another suggestion that could save you money.

Now, conforming to GLOBAL GAP protocols may seem like an unnecessary imposition but all the reasoning behind requirements is logical and you should be doing them anyway when properly managing a safe and hygienic operation. The annual audit becomes a valuable safety check that you are indeed doing just that. It keeps you on your toes and ensures that you are doing your job properly.

CHAPTER TWENTY-FOUR
ESTABLISHING A BREAKEVEN POINT FOR AN AGRICULTURAL ENTERPRISE

A surprising number of aspirant growers going into business say that they would like to begin by erecting a single greenhouse, and if that greenhouse were to prove successful, then they would add on to it and build others, without specifying how many they would add on. Others, when asked, have no idea how to establish a breakeven point - in other words they intend going into business without the slightest notion at what point their business will begin to return a profit. It doesn't take much imagination to realise just how dangerous either one of these positions is.

Firstly, it is imperative for an aspirant business person to know exactly what the costs of running the business are going to be. Failure to realise the extent and number of these costs can mean the difference between success and failure.

It is equally important to estimate a forecast of turnover too for the difference between the two will be the resultant profit (or loss) and form the backbone of The Business Plan.
If the business has already started then costs of running it can be taken from actuals and, likewise with the turnover, figures can be extrapolated and proportioned to an annual basis. If the business has not yet started then estimates need to be carefully and precisely calculated.

In order to do this the expected yields will have to be ascertained and for this you will need the assistance of the seed suppliers so that some reasonable projections can be calculated.

To the expected yields the average estimated selling prices should be applied in order to arrive at a forecast turnover figure.

A single greenhouse is unlikely to be able to produce a turnover that will exceed the costs associated with it so starting small is doomed to failure unless the greenhouse produce is destined for home consumption that will replace normally purchased items.

The next step in establishing the breakeven point is to list all the costs involved in the operation. This is where farmers (who are already operating) stand to develop a profitable hydroponic section because the farm already absorbs some of the overheads such as telephone, rates, electricity, water and other fixed expenses. Obviously, the fewer expenses the hydroponic section has to bear the quicker it will turn a profit. Some expenses will have to be carefully weighed up, such as Global Gap. The cost of an annual audit is linked to the number of different lines a farmer grows so costs can be quite expensive. If one is supplying a supermarket retailer then Global Gap is mandatory and the resultant higher prices and regular large offtake can compensate for the high cost of the Global Gap audit.

Total Expenses:	$ Total	$ Fixed	$ Variable	Estimated Turnover %
Accounting & Bookkeeping Fees	6 500.00	6 500.00		
Bank Charges	10 000.00	10 000.00		
Clothing & Hygiene Staff	3 500.00		3 500.00	0.12
Computer Expenses	4 000.00	4 000.00		
Depreciation included	360 000.00	360 000.00		
Drawings by Members	240 000.00	240 000.00		
Electricity and Water	120 000.00	60 000.00	60 000.00	**2.00**
General Expenses	4 000.00	2 000.00	2 000.00	0.07
Global Gap Audit	10 000.00	10 000.00		
Insurance	25 000.00	25 000.00		
Motor Vehicle Expenses	70 000.00	17 500.00	52 500.00	**1.75**
Nutrients	72 000.00		72 000.00	**2.40**
Pesticides, Insecticides, Sprays	24 000.00		24 000.00	0.80
Bees for Pollination	2 000.00		2 000.00	0.07
Packaging	200 000.00		200 000.00	**6.67**
Postage and Courier	1 000.00	500.00	500.00	0.02
Printing & Stationery	1 000.00	500.00	500.00	
Rates	1 000.00	1 000.00		
Repairs and Maintenance: Buildings/ Electrical/Horticultural/Irrigation	45 000.00	45 000.00		
Refreshments	2 000.00		2 000.00	0.07
Research	1 000.00		1 000.00	0.03
Security	4 000.00	4 000.00		
Seedling Costs	112 000.00		112 000.00	**3.73**
Staff Salaries - normal	400 000.00	53 333.33	346 666.67	**11.56**
Substrate - growing medium	15 000.00		15 000.00	0.50
Telephone & Fax	8 000.00	2 000.00	6 000.00	0.20
Tools & Equipment	8 000.00	2 000.00	6 000.00	0.20
Transport Expenses	2 000.00		2 000.00	0.07
UIF	4 000.00	533.33	3 466.67	0.12
Workmen's Compensation	2 000.00	266.67	1 733.33	0.06
	1 757 000.00	**844 133.33**	**912 866.67**	**30.43**

Estimated turnover — 3 000 000.00

Depreciation 10% p.a over 10 years — See table 3

Source: DaisyFresh Hydroponics

The figures above are estimates relating to a ghost farm. They are relatively accurate and can be used as a template from which to initiate any estimate of breakeven point.

The next step in the exercise is to divide each expense into fixed or variable. The criterion used is:

"What would the business still be liable for if it produced nothing at all?" To give an example, rates would still be payable whether the business produced anything or not. This example is diagnostic. Other expenses can be divided into part fixed and part variable such as motor vehicle expenses where licences are payable whether or not the business produces anything, and the variable element covers the cost of diesel and travelling. Wholly variable expenses are items such as packaging where no expense is incurred if nothing is produced.

Obviously, some of the division is arbitrary and subjective, so the discretion of the business owner or accountant plays a part in deciding the ultimate allocation. When the exercise is complete the % that each expense constitutes of the total estimated turnover can be calculated which will then lead to the total % of the turnover that all the variables comprise. This figure, located on the bottom right of the preceding table, is the ultimate figure that the previous workings have been aiming to establish and will be used in the following table to calculate the breakeven point.

Turnover	500 000	600 000	700 000	800 000	900 000	1 000 000	1 100 000	1 200 000	1 300 000	1 400 000	1 500 000
Fixed Costs	844 133	844 133	844 133	844 133	844 133	844 133	844 133	844 133	844 133	844 133	844 133
Variable Costs (30.4%	152 144	182 573	213 002	243 431	273 860	304 289	334 718	365 147	395 576	426 004	456 433
Fixed & Variable Cost	996 278	1 026 707	1 057 136	1 087 564	1 117 993	1 148 422	1 178 851	1 209 280	1 239 709	1 270 138	1 300 567
Profit/Loss	-496 278	-426 707	-357 136	-287 564	-217 993	-148 422	-78 851	-9 280	60 291	129 862	199 433

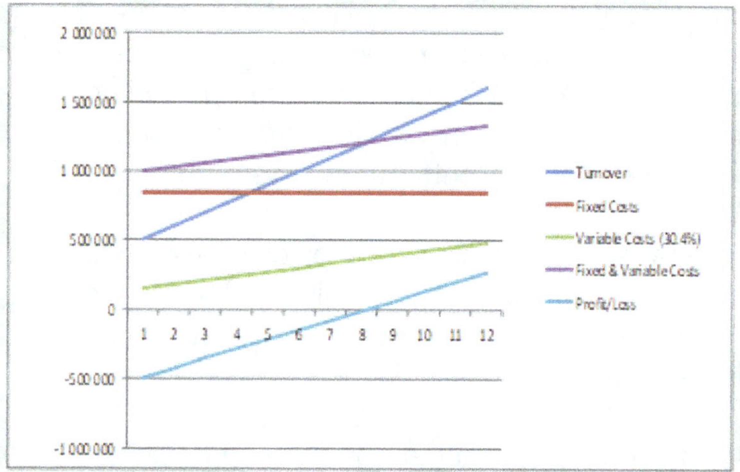

Source: DaisyFresh Hydroponics

Then lay out a number of possible scenarios or 'windows' giving various turnover options and underneath each window insert the fixed cost taken from the bottom of the previous table. Because it's fixed it will always be the same regardless of the turnover figures.

Then insert the product of the variable % of the relevant turnover figure relating to each window. These figures will increase relative to each turnover figure, although the % remains the same.

Now add the fixed costs to the variable costs and you will arrive at total costs. It follows that when comparing total costs with turnover, either a profit or loss is incurred depending upon which figure is the greater.

If costs are greater than turnover then a loss is incurred, and if turnover is greater than total costs then a profit is generated.

The point at which the loss turns into profit is the breakeven point. These values are visually expressed in graph form. For the business, it is obviously preferable to generate a turnover well in excess of breakeven. To generate a turnover at breakeven level will leave the business with little profit, which is, nevertheless though, better than a loss.

The breakeven point is a critical piece of accounting information because it establishes the viability of the business, and is not restricted to hydroponics or farming, but can be used for any business enterprise.

With hydroponics, a target can now be established, dependant on the extent of the business's capability of employing capital. The most straightforward method of deciding how many greenhouses are required to generate a desired turnover is to work out how many plants of a particular cultivar can be accommodated in each greenhouse, multiply that by the expected yield @ the average forecast price to arrive at a forecasted turnover generated by that greenhouse. It doesn't matter if each greenhouse contains a different type of produce as each will contribute whatever its turnover is to the total gross turnover figure. So therefore, by continually adding turnover values per greenhouse one can arrive at and surpass the breakeven point calculated previously.

This is the mathematical way of ensuring that the business will make a profit, rather than starting out with a single greenhouse and if it makes a profit (!) then increasing the size of the growing area.

END OF PART ONE

PART 2

APPLICATIONS IN HYDROPONICS

- Cost-effective hydroponics
- How Hydroponics Saves Water
- How Hydroponics Works
- How to Erect Your Own Greenhouse, Simply and Economically.
- How to Grow Produce in a Hot, Humid Climate
- Hydroponics – a Solution for the Water Shortage
- Hydroponics Training – Why it's Important
- Pitfalls in Hydroponics
- Save Money by Growing Your Own Vegetables
- The 'Breathing' Greenhouse Concept

COST-EFFECTIVE HYDROPONICS

Inflation is rising continually at about 6.25% per annum, and you only have to go to your local supermarket to verify it. Some seasonal vegetables go up and down such as lettuce and tomatoes but when out of season tomatoes are selling for more than $2/kg and lettuces in January and February are going for more than $2 a head then you know you've just seen the signs of inflation, food price inflation.

Here's something you could do to grow your own needs for fruit and vegetables – especially if you have a fondness for growing things - and you can do that quite easily and inexpensively. Hydroponics is the science growing of vegetables and fruit without soil. So, it's not dirty – well, not like you have to go digging around in the soil and wondering whether that soil is rich enough to give your plants the nutrition they need.

Basically, you dissolve two sets of water soluble fertilisers in two separate buckets of water and then pour those buckets into a nutrient tank that feeds your plants. Your plants are held upright by a growing medium, something that imparts no nutrients to the plants, their only job is to keep the plants from falling over and to keep their roots moist. If the roots dry out the plant dies. There are many different types of growing media such as composted pine bark, perlite, LECA pellets, sawdust, wood shavings, rockwool, vermiculite, clinker – the list is quite exhaustive. However, you don't need to be confused by the long list. Composted pine bark is cost-effective, has a pH in line with that recommended for hydroponics and is readily available. You can buy bags of it at your local garden shop or in bulk from

GROMOR or Earth to Earth Organics. You don't need vast tracts of arable land to start a hydroponic garden that will supply you with fruit and vegetables for yourself and family. All you need is somewhere sunny, (therefore preferably north facing or south facing) with a slight slope for the water to drain off.

Source: DaisyFresh Hydroponics

You could start with an area as small as 5m x 3m (15m2) and populate it with vertical growing columns that accommodate 6 times the number of plants per m2 than any other system. Verti-Gro is just such a system.

Developed in USA and patented worldwide the pots are modular and fit into one another to form a column 9 pots high.

This translates into a stack that will house 36 plants and, allowing for walkways, will mean a plant housing population of 30 plants per m2.

So your imaginary plot of 15m2 would house 15/1.2 = 12 stacks of 36 plants each = 432 plants! (Dividing the m2 by 1.2 is a quick way of calculating how many columns (or stacks) can fit into a desired area). You can do this with a hectare; 10 000 m2 divided by 1.2 = 8333 stacks x 36 plants each = 300 000 plants!

You'll need to buy a header/collection tank to house the nutrient water, and for a small area of 12 columns a 500-litre tank will do, and dig it into the ground leaving 150mm protruding. They are available quite reasonably from Hardware suppliers or tank manufacturers. Into this you'll need to place a submersible pump that can pump the nutrients to the plants. The Chinese make a good one called SHIMGE and a 0.25kw submersible will do the job and costs about $125 from the local agents.

Recirculating the used nutrient water (known as leachate) will cut down the costs of fertilisers and water so to do that you'll have to get 12 by 10L buckets from a plastic shop and fill them with gravel. The columns are erected on top of the stones and held upright by 2m lengths of 12mm square tubing which you can pick up from a scrapyard or a steel supplier if you prefer to buy new.

Now link the buckets to the tank by drilling a hole in the buckets and inserting a 15mm LDPE tube into the hole, with a grommet to stop leaks. Tubing and grommets are available from specialist hydroponic suppliers. The LDPE pipe does not need to be longer than about 30 cm and should be connected to a 50mm PVC white plastic drainage tube which you connect to the tank. LDPE 25mm feeder tubing can be used to connect the pump to the tops of the columns via arrow drippers and plastic connectors.

The columns will need to be stabilised by tying the tops of the metal centre poles to points on the periphery of your growing area. This can be the side of a house or building on the one side and wooden poles inserted into the ground on the other. If you are growing herbs or strawberries that prefer full sun you don't need to use any shade cloth for their protection. However, if you have monkeys in your area you'll have to protect your crop with wire, either chicken wire or weldmesh. Tomatoes will need protection from the monkeys and you'll need to shade them from the very hot sun with shade cloth of 30% or 40% green or black.

It's a good idea to get yourself an EC meter to measure the strength of the nutrients you'll be supplying your plants. Salad greens like about 1.5EC and tomatoes about 2.5EC so bear in mind that with this difference in nutrient strength it would not be a good idea to grow them both together unless you had a dual parallel feeding system with two tanks and two pumps. Alternatively, you would have to grow them alternately. EC meters are supplied by local instrument suppliers.

If you feel that erecting your own greenhouse is too much like hard work you can get a hydroponic supplies company to build you a wooden pole and shadecloth structure tailor made to suit your space, and also supply all the accessories that go inside.

Alternatively, you could ask a hydroponic supplies company to erect a plastic and metal lean-to using the side of the house as one anchor point.

Source: DaisyFresh Hydroponics

Source: DaisyFresh Hydroponics

CHAPTER TWENTY-SIX
HOW HYDROPONICS SAVES WATER

Before delving into how hydroponics can save water we firstly need to understand how hydroponics works.

Hydroponics is the growing of plants in nutrient solutions, with or without sand, gravel or other inert medium to provide mechanical support. The main difference between hydroponics and traditional soil-based agriculture is that with hydroponics the nutrition comes from water soluble fertilisers rather than the soil; thus, in hydroponics there is no soil.

In hydroponics plants can be grown using a number of different systems. Nutrient film technique (NFT) uses long PVC troughs or channels equipped with a fitted lid into which holes are made. The plants hang suspended through the holes and a film of nutrient water is passed underneath them over the bottom of the channel.

Similarly, sand or gravel filled beds can be used to house the plants. The sand (river sand, not soil) or gravel is housed in a plastic lined trough made by using wooden poles or bricks. The nutrient water is passed through the growing medium from one end to the other (the bed is set at a slight slope).

Vertical growing systems house the plants in medium-filled pots that fit integrally into one another forming a column 1.8m high. The nutrient water is fed into the top pot and percolates down through holes in the pots from one pot to the next.

There is an enormous space saving using this method.

The bag system uses dual extruded plastic bags to hold the chosen medium, black on the inside to inhibit weed growth and white on the outside to reflect the maximum amount of light. The nutrient water passes out through holes in the bottom of the bag and collected in a bucket from where it is returned to the header tank.

There are other growing systems used in hydroponics but the four referred to are the most popular. In every case the nutrient water is housed firstly in a header tank, then fed to the plants using polyethylene tubing and collected again after use and returned to the header tank for continued recycling. The nutrients tend to go out of balance after a couple of weeks and salt from the water source also can build up in the system so it's a recommendation to empty the header tank once a fortnight and dump the contents over the garden, lawn or other needy area.

This, then, is the crux of how water can be saved using hydroponics. For 13 days water is re-circulated and used over and over again – only on the 14th day is it dumped, and then it's not a complete waste as it can be put to good use in other non-hydroponic applications. The water used in hydroponics is confined only to the water that the plant uses as it draws the nutrient water up into its system through osmosis and the water passes out via evaporation through the plant leaves.

Nutrient water whilst being fed to the plants is not exposed to sunlight and consequent loss through evaporation.
Consider just how much water is used in agriculture, especially with spray irrigation. Huge pivots are used to spray large volumes of water on to massive expanses, all of which are exposed to the sunlight and consequent evaporation. Then, in addition, 99% of the irrigation water flows past the root zone and is lost to the water table – a huge waste.

Drip-fed irrigation uses polyethylene tubing submerged under the soil surface to feed the plants. In addition, a thin film of plastic mulch is used to conserve moisture in the soil by protecting it from the sunlight, so this method precludes loss through evaporation, but there is nevertheless a loss of water flowing past the roots and back into the water table.

Because of the difference in the two forms of growing plants, hydroponics uses less than one third of the water compared to traditional agriculture, which is a strong factor in its favour in a water-stressed country. Already parts of the world are in a dire drought so we need to become more circumspect about how we can save water. Harvesting water from roof run-off is another ideal way water can be conserved and is ideal for use in hydroponics except where roof tops are near the sea which can deposit large amounts of salt on them via sea spray.

CHAPTER TWENTY-SEVEN
HOW HYDROPONICS WORKS

Hydroponics began in the 1930's in the USA as an outgrowth of the culture techniques used by plant physiologists in plant nutrition experiments in the USA. It did not begin with the Hanging Gardens of Babylon as many might incorrectly pre-suppose. There were no compound chemicals available then and at best the Hanging Gardens were a series of cleverly constructed water channels down which the water flowed thus watering all the plants in soil-based systems from top to bottom.

Hydro – Greek for water and 'ponos' meaning work gives us the sense that hydroponics means to work in water.

In a nutshell the basic difference between hydroponics and traditional soil-based agriculture lies in the fact that in hydroponics the nutrient food for the plants comes from water soluble nutrients whereas in agriculture the nutrients come from the soil. Thus, hydroponics can be said to be the growing of plants in nutrient solutions, with or without sand, gravel or other inert medium to provide mechanical support. In hydroponics there is no soil.

---

[1] See image on page 2

Having established that fact one might be tempted to assume that hydroponics is a much simpler way of growing plants than growing in the soil, but this is not totally true. Hydroponics is a meld of chemical engineering and agriculture and (apart from nutrition) other aspects, such as pest and diseases, and the preferences of the plant for more or less light, remain the same.

Plant nutrition in hydroponics is based upon the premise that all the nutrients that are required for the plant's growth throughout its life cycle will be supplied in the same proportions that the plant will take up. Developmental science has established that there are 16 different elements that need to be supplied to the plant to maintain growth, development and survival, or put another way, for foliar development, flowering and fruiting. These elements are divided into 6 macro nutrients (where the minerals are absorbed in large quantities) 7 micro nutrients (where the minerals are absorbed in minute quantities) and three gases.

Minerals are measured in parts per million (ppm's) and these are expressed in grams per million cubic centimetres of water. 1m cc's of water is 1 Litre so ppm's = g/L in the case of macro nutrients and milligrams (one thousandth of a gram) per 1m cc's water in the case of micro nutrients or mg/L. Developmental science has established certain bandwidths within which the minerals should fall and they are broadly as follows:

ELEMENT	Parts per million bandwidths
Nitrogen (N)	100 – 450
Phosphorous (P)	10 – 100
Potassium (K)	100 – 750
Magnesium (Mg)	20 – 95
Calcium (Ca)	70 – 350
Sulphur (S)	20 – 250
Iron (Fe)	1 – 6
Manganese (Mn)	0.8 – 4
Boron (B)	0.3 – 0.8
Zinc (Zn)	0.2 – 0.5
Molybdenum (Mo)	0.05 – 0.2
Copper (Cu)	0.05 – 0.1
Chlorine (Cl)	0.01 – 0.02

Perfect nutrition results in perfect plants

The reason for such precision in the balance of nutrients is to avoid toxicity or deficiency in the nutrient mix.

Thus, contrary to what occurs in soil, the plants are supplied in just the correct proportions that they need resulting in perfectly balanced nutrition, the exact requirements of the plant resulting in optimal growth and high quality produce. If the produce is perfect then so are the availability of vitamins and minerals also at their maximum. In soil and organic growing the plant nutrients are not perfectly balanced often resulting in poor nutrition and slow growth. Yields are reduced and growth is stunted with consequent attacks by pests and diseases as they always attack a weak plant first.

When growing in soil farmers must have their soils analysed to establish what minerals are missing and add lime to them to balance the pH level and fertilisers to fill in the missing minerals. Completely balanced nutrient levels are not always possible when farming in soil.

Most fertiliser companies supply their nutrient mixes in the form of a cocktail or blend of nutrients containing all the minerals except Calcium Nitrate which is supplied separately. This is to prevent the Calcium and Sulphur reacting together and forming Calcium Sulphate which sets up like epoxy-resin when mixed together in concentrated form.

pH measures the number of Hydrogen ions present in a solution and is important in Hydroponics because the minerals are absorbed by the plant more readily when the pH is between 5.5 and 6.0 (7.0 is neutral). A hydroponic enthusiast should get a hand held pH and EC meter combined – Hanna instruments make a good one.

It's important, before starting a hydroponic venture, to get a proper education in hydroponics. This will save you a lot of money and prevent you from making costly mistakes.
DaisyFresh Hydroponics offers an online course – go to
daisyfreshhydroponics@gmail.com
or
www.daisyfreshhydroponics.com

CHAPTER TWENTY-EIGHT
HOW TO ERECT YOUR OWN GREENHOUSE, SIMPLY AND ECONOMICALLY.

The two most important things you must do before you start are:

Check the water quality and have it analysed. Na Cl must be very low. The water should be pure and free of dissolved solids. The ground should be clear of trees and should be downwards sloping towards the sun source – North in the Southern Hemisphere and South in the Northern hemisphere. Flat ground is also acceptable.

Marking out the ground:

Firstly, you need to decide how large you want to build your greenhouse. If you use the Verti-Gro system bear in mind that you can average about 30 plants per m2 with it. Other systems such as gravel beds work out at only about 4-6 plants per m2 and are therefore much more costly. Decide what you wish to grow first and then work out the space that you'll be requiring, depending upon the system you choose.

Make sure that the long sides of the structure will face east and west and the short sides face north and south.

You can opt for any shape you prefer, but square or rectangular shapes are the most practical. Stay away from circular, or polygon shapes as they tend to be more complicated. You can choose from 3m x 5m or multiples of that size up to 18 x 30. Much larger than that becomes more impractical when it comes to finding long enough roof battens.

Mark out the size of the structure by pegging some yellow builders cord into the ground with 6" nails. Make sure than the corners are 90 degrees by using the 3, 4, 5 method. Pythagoras theorem stated that the square of the hypotenuse equals the square of the remaining two sides. Thus 3 squared plus 4 squared equals 5 squared. So, 9 + 16 = 25. Once you have your triangle correct, line it up with the northerly/southerly direction and complete the other three corners in the same way.

Dig holes in the ground at the corners and every 2.5 – 3.0 m in between. E.g. 5m divided by 2 spaces = 1 pole leaving 2.5m on either side. 3.0m = no poles required in between and so on. 10m x 6.0m = 4 spaces (three poles @ 2.5m apart x 3 spaces of 2.0m (two poles).

If your structure is to be permanent it's a good idea to concrete the corner poles into the ground. Poles should be CCA treated (Chromium, Copper and Arsenic) and 3.6m in length. The diameter of the corner poles should be 100 – 125mm in diameter and the in-between poles 80 – 100mm. Horizontal poles should be 80 – 100mm. and equal to the distance you have left between the uprights. Depth of the uprights should be 600mm on the upper side and 550mm on the lower side.

Attach a cable tie to the spade at the appropriate depths to ensure the holes are correct. Make sure the upright poles are all of equal length.

At the same time as you are digging the holes for the poles you should dig a 1m x 1m hole for the tank. It should be equal to the height of the tank measured from the shoulder of the tank to the floor and should be at the lowest point round the structure.

Source: DaisyFresh Hydroponics

Erecting the Structure:
The horizontal poles should be level and uprights should be vertical. This can be checked with a spirit level. For the uprights don't forget to check the planes in both directions N-S and E-W. An extra pole has to be included for the gate.

The easiest way to fix the horizontal poles is to purchase L profile metal pole brackets from a good hardware supplier or pole outlet. Measure the diameter end of the pole you are going to put into position, then affix the brackets with coach screws allowing space for the pole so that when in position the pole will be flush with the tops of the uprights. Then the horizontal poles can be dropped into position and affixed with coach screws.

Source: DaisyFresh Hydroponics

If the holes have been dug correctly the 600mm holes on the one side will be slightly deeper than the 550mm holes on the other, thus allowing for a slightly sloping roof for the water to run off.

The ground can now be cleared and should be graded with a slight slope towards the hole for the tank.

Next you must brace the uprights against strong winds with wire stays.

Cut 2m iron stakes into halves of 1m each and drive them into the ground at 45 degrees to the vertical, leaning away from the greenhouse. They should be hammered in with a 2kg hammer, and only 100mm should be left protruding. Attach a 3.8mm wire to the stake and cut it about 500mm from the upright it is going to support. Wrap a length of the same wire around the upright so the loop goes around the horizontal as well, thus preventing the loop from slipping down the pole.

Twist the wire connected to the top of the upright so that it cannot undo and connect both ends to each other with a wire fence tensioner.

Then connect each upright to the upright on the opposite side of the structure, again tensioning the wire with a fence tensioner. It is not necessary to tighten this tensioner up more than just to take up the slack in the wire. A major part of the tension will come from the outer tensioners.

Do not over tighten the outer stays until their opposite numbers are in position. Then tighten each one a little at a time so that the one does not pull the other one over. The tension on each wire should balance the other so that they are in equilibrium. This goes for all the stay wires you need to put up; each corner will require two stays, one for each direction NS and EW. Inter poles only require a single stay. In principle, each pole will be connected under tension to an opposite number, so that when all the tensioners are tightened all the poles will be under tension and supported by the stays. This will ensure that your structure can withstand gales and rogue winds of more than 100 k.p.h.

Immediately you have completed the wire stays you are advised to wrap them in reflective tape to prevent people from being throttled, especially at night; the ground stakes should be covered with 75mm long x 50mm white piping to prevent ankle injuries. You can hammer these protectors on with a rubber mallet and they will deform to the shape of the stakes and stay securely on.

Source: DaisyFresh Hydroponics

You can now erect the roof; connect the battens across the roof so that the glass fibre runs downwards but across the battens. Connect the battens with 100mm threaded roof nails and washers. Leave at least 40cm between each batten so that the roofer can later get between them to drill and hammer on the glass fibre sheets.

If you'd like to cover the roof with shade cloth you can wire on a trellis to support it, bearing in mind that by so doing you will not make your greenhouse waterproof, although you might save on the cost of battens and glass fibre. Glass fibre can be opaque or red if you can get it, for optimally fast plant growth. You will find that self-tapping bolts are the easiest to use to affix the roof sheets. A little encouragement with a hammer will make a pilot hole, and the self-tapping bolt should be used in conjunction with a rubber–lined washer.

Next you need to decide how secure you wish to make your greenhouse. If you live in a monkey populated area (whether two legged or four legged) you will be well advised to erect weld mesh round the sides of the structure. To do this properly you must first erect three strands of the 2.5mm wire between each outer pole; one on the floor and two more 1 metre from each other. The top strand will thus be 2m from the floor. Each strand should be tensioned with wire fence tensioners between each pole (although it is possible to by-pass the centre poles with a small greenhouse and only use a single fence tensioner). If you are erecting a greenhouse of more than 5m along one of the sides then more fence tensioners will be required along that distance.

The weldmesh can now be cut to size and attached to the support wires with light weight 1.0mm wire. Attachments will need to be every 30cm to be effective. The top of the weldmesh can be attached to the horizontal poles with U-nails. It's not advisable to try and erect the weldmesh in a single piece that goes completely around the four sides of the greenhouse at once. Weldmesh is springy and trying to erect it all at once will result in more difficulties than any saving obtained. Rather, measure each side and cut to size, snipping off any excess ends once it is in position. Don't leave spiky ends for they will catch on and damage the shadecloth when this is placed into position.

A cheaper option than expensive weldmesh is to use chicken wire in order to save money. However, the downside to this suggestion is that the chicken wire rusts more quickly and is more easily penetrated by interlopers. If you want your greenhouse free of problems and to last for a reasonably long time I would suggest that you spend a little extra on the weldmesh. 3m wide weldmesh is available that will cover the sides of the structure without having to cut the height to size.

Once the weldmesh is in position you can now affix the shadecloth to it; cable ties (black for UV resistance) are ideal for quick connections and in no time the structure is complete with shade protecting cloth. If you have to trim the shadecloth anywhere do remember that shadecloth frays so you will have to use a candle, and quickly and lightly draw the edges of the shadecloth over the flame in order to seal it and prevent it from fraying.

Finally, you will need to prevent grass from the strimmers from entering the greenhouse through the shade cloth so you'll need to erect a polypropylene woven skirt around your structure. This needs to be only 50cm wide and you can tack it in position top and bottom with nylon line. You'll need two people to do this, one on the inside and the other on the outside, to pass the needle back and forth.

Preparing the Interior for the Growing System:

Before fitting the plastic floor, dig shallow trenches to accommodate the drainage piping. This is white rigid 50 mm PVC and if laid with the soil just covering the pipe will result in a smooth obstacle-free floor. When connecting the buckets, drill holes in the white 50 mm piping to accommodate the 15 x 19mm LDPE tubing.

Holes can be drilled through the white plastic floor but care should be taken not to damage the plastic. Plastic white repair tape is available to cover accidents. Holes are drilled in the buckets about 5cm from the bottom and rubber grommets are inserted into these holes to prevent nutrient water from leaking out. Short lengths of 15mm LDPE tubing are cut and inserted into the grommets and the drainage piping. can now be filled with gravel stones.

Your greenhouse is now complete and ready for you to erect the growing pots or bags ready for the plants. If you use Verti-Gro pots you can erect them one to a stack allowing the plants to grow outwards and downwards. Determinate varieties should be chosen for this purpose.

Source: DaisyFresh Hydroponics

The stacks are kept upright by 2m x 15mm steel poles primed with NH4, and prevented from going down into the stones by wooden blocks. The pots are held in position on top of 50mm white tubing and the water is collected from the pot by means of a funnel. This has the additional advantage of allowing the stack to be turned through 180 degrees to obtain an even distribution of light should this be necessary in low light areas.

The Verti-Gro system is highly practical and effective and allows for a high number of plants to be grown in a relatively small area. The structure below, for example, measures 15 m2, yet accommodates 23 columns, each with places for 8 plants, making a total of 184 plants or 12.3 plants per m2.

Source: DaisyFresh Hydroponics

Before planting the seedlings it is advisable to disinfect the whole system with SPOREKILL and fit a foot bath filled with disinfectant in the doorway so that anyone entering the greenhouse is obliged to walk through it. A spray bottle hanging from the overhead wire above the door is also recommended for sanitising hands.

Guttering is not obligatory and does add to the cost but is highly convenient and practical especially when walking round the greenhouse on the lower side during the rain in order to work on the tank and load nutrients in the system.

Next the water distribution system can be fitted and connected. Using 25 mm black LDPE tubing, connect a submersible pump placed in a 500 litre tank in the ground with the main nutrient distribution tubing. This is then connected in turn with 15mm LDPE tubing which is run along the tops of the columns and connected in position by attaching it to 3,8 mm tensioned wire strung along the tops of the pots for the purpose. Cable ties make ideal items for attaching the tubing to the wires. Next drill the tubing with 2,5 mm holes and press the 2 litre/hour drippers into the drilled holes. Attach the t-pieces to the drippers and the micro tubing to the t-pieces procured for the purpose; in turn attach the micro tubing to the arrow heads.

Source: DaisyFresh Hydroponics

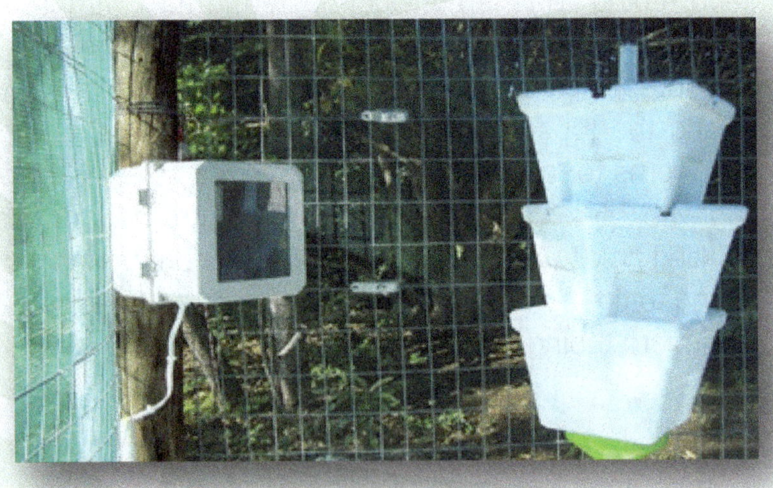

Source: DaisyFresh Hydroponics

Fill the top 2 buckets with 12 mm composted pine bark (wetted first with sterilising agent) and place some fly netting, duly cut to size, in the bottom of the lower bucket to catch any extraneous matter and prevent it from going into the tank. Shimge (China) make a very good economical submersible pump but its capacity for water delivery far exceeds the 4m head required for this installation (taking into account the fact that the tank is sunk in the ground by approximately 1m (see left hand bottom corner of picture on page 146) plus 2m to reach the top of the columns, plus a 1m cracking pressure required to break through the drippers) so a by-pass valve should be installed to reduce the workload on the pump and prolong its life. This enables the water to be channelled back into the tank, aerating the nutrient water at the same time. The valve used to achieve this is used to control the amount of pressure required to get nutrient water to the drippers with sufficient flow. Also advisable is for you to fit a discharge valve to enable you to dump the nutrient water every two weeks.

You can fit your nutrient fertigation system with a time clock to do the switching on and off for you, and you should also fit a nylon stocking to the return pipe going into the tank to prevent further foreign matter from entering the tank.
Finally, don't forget to insulate the black LDPE tubing with Alucushion thus preventing the sun from boiling the water prior to feeding the plants.

CHAPTER TWENTY-NINE
HOW TO GROW PRODUCE IN A HOT, HUMID CLIMATE

Hot, humid climates present unique problems to hydroponic growers, especially in summer.

Many people fall for the salesman's ruse that plants must have protection from the weather and therefore the best way of protecting them is by covering them with a sheet of plastic. The net result of this action is that the sun can heat up the inside of the tunnel to 55°C or more, together with extreme humidity. Both these factors make it impossible for plants to grow and the countryside is littered with empty plastic covered tunnels where gullible aspirant hydroponic farmers have failed.

Attempting to cool down the tunnels with water is fruitless and the reason why is supplied by the example in the following table:

DISADVANTAGE OF PLASTIC IN HIGH HUMIDITY AREAS

Temperature	Humidity (rH)	Efficacy
36°c	90%	10%

To measure the efficacy of water cooling take the % humidity and subtract it from 100%. The resultant figure gives you the effective potential for cooling; in this case it's 10%. Then subtract the 10% from the ambient temperature of 36C and the net result is 32.4°C. As previously pointed out, if nothing grows over 30°C then this attempt to cool down the tunnel with water is quite fruitless, resulting merely in a waste of electricity and water with nothing achieved.

The principle shown here is the same for any relationship between temperature and humidity and it's useful to be able to establish the potential for cooling by this method before wasting money on expensive plastic sheeting and water cooling apparatus. The same applies to misters.

Now that we've dispelled the myth that plastic sheet covering is the best way to protect plants what method would we recommend for their protection that would create a cool environment for them in which to grow? To arrive at this conclusion we would draw your attention to the plant nurseries that have been growing seedlings hydroponically for decades. They do this very successfully under shadecloth, held erect by wooden poles and wire and this is the proven method of grow-ing small sensitive plants. The more shade you require for your plants the higher percentage of shadecloth will be necessary. For tender plants and those that prefer full shade such as lettuce, apply 60% -70% shade cloth depending on whether you live in a hot or very hot area. Peppers would require 50% - 60% as they are most prone to sunburn. Vanilla would need 90% as they prefer nearly full shade. Each vegetable has its own preference.

However if you can provide the plants with a cool environment and grow them successfully then you should be able to command a good price for them. They are easy to grow in winter as they are a cool-loving crop so the supply is plentiful then and the prices at rock-bottom.

There are many other essential things you can do to supply a cool environment for your plants in a sub-tropical or tropical zone. Bear in mind that the whole objective is to keep the leaf surface temperature and the roots as cool as possible. You can:

• Bury the nutrient water tanks in the ground leaving 15cm protruding so that flood waters do not enter the tanks and contaminate the nutrient water. This will insulate the tanks and keep them cool.
• Paint the tops of the tanks silver to reflect any sunlight that might reach them.
• Cover the tank area with a high % shadecloth (90% if possible) as this will help to keep them cool. A shade cloth box is recommended.
• Cool the water down with a water chiller – this is essential to keep the roots cool. If the ambient is around 30°C or more you can cool the water to about 20°C or even lower. Take the temperature of the roots with a thermometer and try and get them to as near as 24°C as possible. You may have to cool the water down quite considerably as it will tend to heat up on the way to the plants.

• Bury all exposed tubing possible and wrap exposed tubing with Alucushion or silver paper. Alucushion is like silver bubble wrap so it does a great job.
• Make sure that your floors are covered with dual extruded plastic sheeting – white up for light reflection and black down for weed inhibition.
• Install a couple of high speed fans at the prevailing wind end of the tunnel and a couple in the middle. This will help to keep the humidity down.

If you grow with Verti-Gro polystyrene pots, not only will you fit six times the number of plants in the same space but the pots insulate the roots by 4/5 degrees, making them cooler in summer and warmer in winter.

CHAPTER THIRTY
HYDROPONICS - A SOLUTION TO THE WATER SHORTAGE

A dramatic new phenomenon has entered the world geography scenario, that of global warming, or as it has recently been more correctly called, climate change. Climate change is having a marked effect on countries the world over, with dry or poorly irrigated countries suffering even further from lack of water, and countries with more than adequate water resources being inundated. The ice caps' melting is further exacerbating the situation by raising sea levels. Higher sea levels of warmer water worsen the situation even further.

Anthony Turton, a world acclaimed water and energy specialist, was dismissed from his position some years ago, when he was on the point of presenting a paper revealing just how acute his country's own water position is and is going to be. Perhaps this was a quotable case of 'killing the messenger who brings the bad news' but the fact that he wasn't able to present the paper and reveal to the public the gravity of our situation reflects negatively and sadly on our ability to face reality and do something about it. Most of us continue unaware that our water situation is indeed dire and many farmers are wondering, hoping that the government will come to their aid and supply them with water because they 'feed the nation' and the nation cannot go without food.

Sadly, because, like the frog immersed into cold water which is then brought to the boil and dies, the situation changes gradually; the government leaves farming to the farmers, as can be seen by over 90% of Africa's farms now becoming net exporters of food.

One can rapidly appreciate the worsening situation for us from the prediction made by the World Meteorological Organization as depicted below.

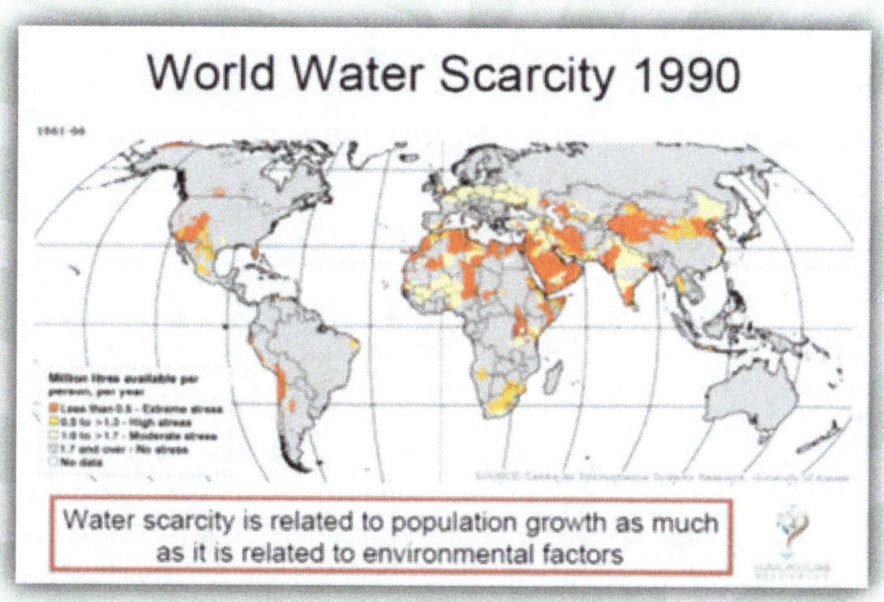

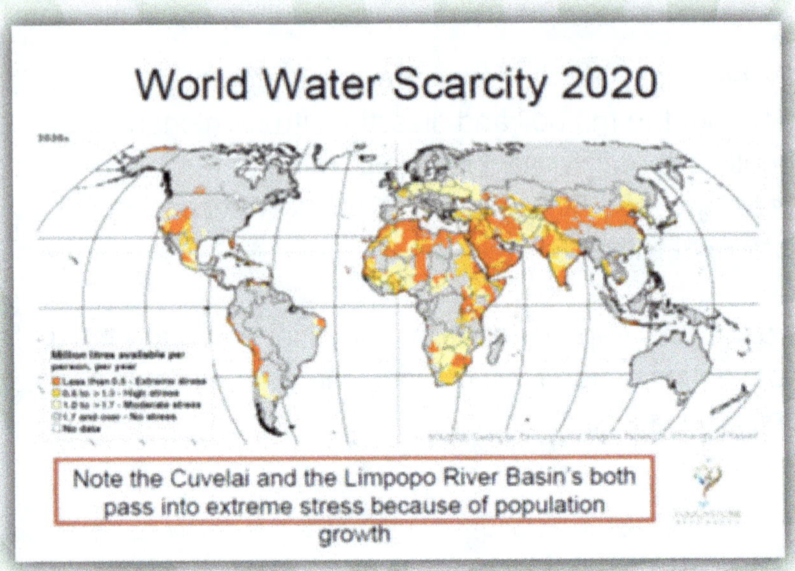

Source: Maps and table by Touchstone Resources

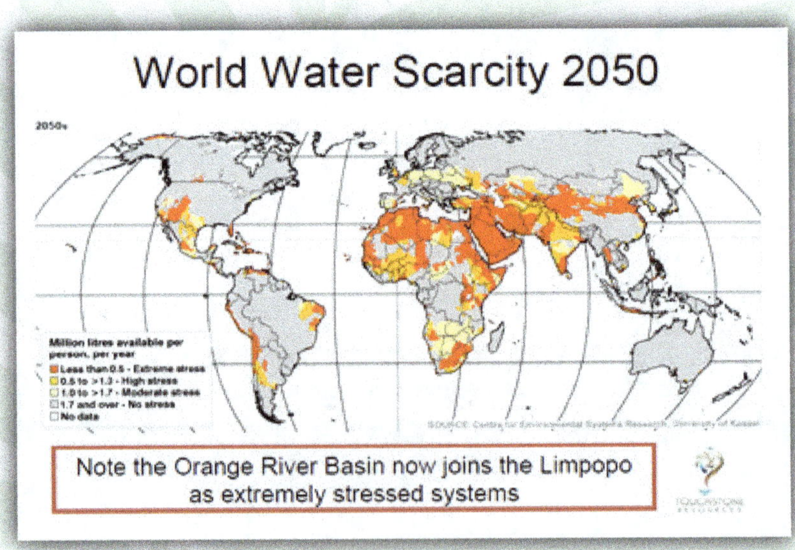

Water Crowding as a Concept

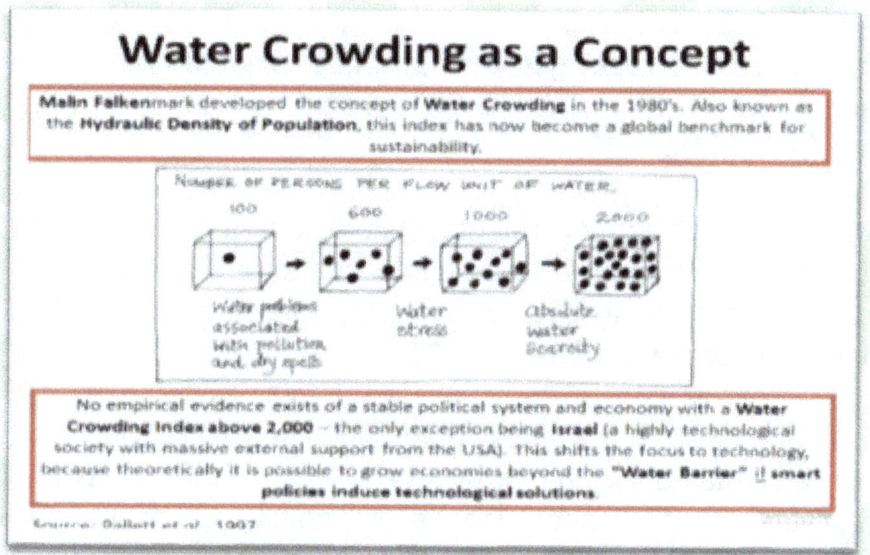

Source: Maps and table by Touchstone Resources

The problem with climate change where it reduces the annual rainfall in an already dry country is that all the dam building that one may construct will not alter by a single drop the amount of water that falls (or rather doesn't fall) from the sky. When reverse osmosis machines are installed they are often neglected and left to fall into disrepair.

This leads me to the main topic. Agriculture uses vast amounts of water for overhead irrigation, all of which (other than the small amount that the plants soak up) is lost to the water table irretrievably. Farmers who have dams and rivers that don't dry up can use large amounts of water to this end with relatively little penalty, but sooner or later when the effects of climate change dry up the rivers and dams what will they then do? By that stage it will be too late to take any action that will provide an immediate solution to the problem, and the governments will not be sympathetic to trucking in large quantities of water for agriculture when other sectors of the community still don't have any for drinking.

A possible solution for fruit and vegetable farmers would be to look now at alternative ways of growing produce that is cost-effective and less wasteful of precious water. One of those ways is hydroponics.

In a given system that uses about 1000 litres per 30 000 plants per feed, the consumption does vary because the transpiration rate varies in accordance with the temperature and the humidity. (1600 drippers @ 2 litres per hour for 30 minutes = 1600 litres of which more than half is returned for re-use). So an average of five feeds per day would consume 5000 litres. On the assumption that 60 000 plants occupy 1 hectare, the system uses the equivalent of 10 000 litres, whereas watering 1 hectare of plants for 15 minutes per day in the open field, uses (from experience) 30 000 litres of water per day all of which is lost to the water table.

For farmers using their own rivers, dams and boreholes this wastage is bad enough but when paying for water from Municipalities where no allowance is made for agriculture the cost (to market gardeners for example) is crippling. Where water is in short supply from natural sources (see maps above) farmers run the risk of being dried up out of business.
So as a rule of thumb we can assume that a re-circulating hydroponic system will use approximately one third of the water used in the open field (all other things being equal).

The main advantage with hydroponics is for fruit and vegetable farmers where items like lettuce, spinach, herbs, strawberries, celery, tomatoes, brinjals, capsicums, pineapples (and many other plants) can be grown. Where fruit grows on trees and crops extend over vast areas, such as sugar cane, science has not yet invented a system where these crops can be accommodated hydroponically.

Learning How to Do Hydroponics:

Hydroponics is not rocket science and can be mastered relatively easily especially by anyone already involved in horticulture or agriculture. If you already know how a plant grows and what action to take to eliminate pests and diseases you are already halfway there. A cost-effective course will teach prospective growers how to grow successfully with hydroponics and how to generate another income stream. *This last fact is very important for all farmers because they can start with a small piece of land now and develop another source of income without waiting for water sources to dry up completely.* Don't wait until your water sources have dried up - act now while the going is still relatively good and prepare for the drier times to come. It's just like storing up feed in summer for the leaner winter.

WHAT YOU NEED IN ORDER TO GROW IN HYDROPONICS:

You'll need a source of pure water (not brackish or salt laden and have it analysed before you begin) and some flattish land. (Slightly sloping North or South, i.e. sunwards, is best).

Then, electricity to drive the pumps, and the various accessories required depending on which system you choose. You do not require expensive tunnels and can erect a growing area with gum poles and shade cloth, provided the structure is well anchored against high winds. These more cost-effective structures are about one-tenth the cost of tunnels and puts hydroponics within the reach of every farmer. If you decide to grow vertically you'll need one-sixth of the land to grow the same number of plants compared with normal agriculture.

CHAPTER THIRTY-ONE
HYDROPONICS
TRAINING - WHY IT'S IMPORTANT

Would you go to an unqualified Doctor if you were ill? Do you know of any CEO of a Company that isn't qualified or trained for the position? Many people might regard these questions as frivolous but the same can be said of the application of hydroponics, which is a science all of its own and a meld of chemistry and agriculture. Imagine trying to make a pair of good shoes without having been trained in the art.

Full blown advanced courses in hydroponics can take 300 hours of study and generally form part of a Diploma, which will give one a better idea of just how much material there is on the subject.

If one is contemplating setting up a hydroponic venture of one's own it makes sense to ensure that as much knowledge as possible is accumulated beforehand, in order to avoid costly mistakes on the one hand and also to maximise yields on the other.

A good hydroponics course should cover the following topics:
• Plants, plant physiology, learning how they work
• EC, ppm's and pH – what do they mean and how to use them
• Nutrition – learn the parameters for optimal growth
• Systems – the various ways that can be used to grow plants
•Systems – from fully automated to manual controls
• Systems – run to waste or re-circulating systems

- Climatic preferences for the plants
- Site Selection, criteria for optimum yields
- Growing media
- Tunnel coverings – which is best for the climate
    - Plastic or shade cloth?
    - Tunnels or Gum Poles?
    - Multispans
- Pack house and Pump house requirements – do's and don'ts
- Pests and Diseases – good management, biological controls
- Organics : how to be organic - hydroponic
- Hygiene and Packaging
- Transportation
- GlobalGap
- Setting a Breakeven Point for Your Business

Even a cursory examination of these topics will reveal a minefield of possible areas where costly mistakes can be made, resulting in high school fees arising as crops are either lost, or yields are depressed below breakeven point due to malnutrition, pests, diseases or any other of a plethora of different reasons.

It's a good idea to attend a Hydroponics School where all of these subjects are covered during a two-day course. Courses which are held in a rural environment at a congenial Conference Centre where lunches and teas are provided giving the delegates every opportunity for learning as much as possible during the period are often preferred. Where delegates from afar can stay at a Conference Centre this further eases the burden of travel.

Many delegates when completing a course are significantly surprised by how much they learned and how much they had to 'unlearn'. This unlearning process is generally caused by wrong assumptions or misinformation they might have gleaned from amateurs contributing to the Internet.

Delegates should be taken on a tour of a working hydroponic farm to see in practice what they previously learned in theory.

CHAPTER THIRTY-TWO
PITFALLS IN HYDROPONICS

It's worthwhile examining some of the shortcomings of the hanging bag system and the dangers of unscrupulous franchisors. These are two very real dangers for potential hydroponics farmers, but there are many others too of which the inexperienced hydroponics farmer may not be aware.

Before dealing with those others however, it may be worthwhile examining with a little more detail the reasons associated with the failure of the hanging bag system (which gives other successful vertical systems a bad name) and other failed franchises.

The mechanical collapse of the hanging bag system was a small part of the real reasons why it doesn't work. It was unfortunate that the steel wire employed to keep the bandolier erect was not sufficiently strong or sufficiently well anchored to do the job. More likely, too many hanging bags were suspended from a single wire that could practically have been supported by that system. This is a common mistake made by designers and constructors of that system. They assume that any number of bags can be placed side by side without due regard to the physical tolerances of the wire and its anchoring system.

What is more important is that no attention is given to the plant's light requirements and it is often incorrectly assumed that the supply of light is infinite. This is not so. Light, measured in Lux units varies in from country to country from about 650 units during midday in summer to less than 400 in winter. The supply of light is not infinite, and once more than about 30 plants per square metre are crowded into the same space there is not then enough light to go around and growth suffers. Linked to the light distribution factor is the physical orientation of the bandolier. Most hydroponic systems are sited in such a way that they face North or South, so that as the sun makes its way from east to west during the day the spread of light is evenly dispersed over all the plants. With the bandolier system this is impossible as the system itself shades 50% of the plants from the sunlight, depending whether it is morning or afternoon. In other words, in the morning only one side of the bandolier receives the sunlight (the other is in shade) and in the afternoon the reverse side receives the sunlight. A Bandolier system can only ever therefore, receive 50% of the sunlight that other successful systems can provide. If the bandolier system were inadvertently sited east to west, the southern side of the row would receive no sunlight at all. A comparison with the VERTI-GRO vertical growing system reveals that the latter (that consists of nine polystyrene pots that are fitted into one another to form a vertical column receives light from 360 degrees and the columns are sited from between 800mm to 1200mm from each other in such a way that wrap-around light is allowed access to the plants from any direction). No more than 30 plants per square metre are fitted. A standard 8 x 30 tunnel can accommodate 7200 plants using the VERTI-GRO system.

As important as the question of light access to the plants, is the ability of the bag to distribute nutrients to the plants evenly and quickly. The normal size bags can hold 1000 cc of earth, or medium. Depending on the root system of the plant, this is generally too small simply because the bags are suspended and the plastic comprising the bag exerts a pressure on the medium, thus compressing it to an extent that eventually little or no nutrient can make its way through the system. The roots of the plants compound the problem by searching for nutrient and, as a rule, extend throughout the bag compartment thus further blocking any flow of nutrient. The plants eventually become pot-bound and then die from under-nutrition or thirst. Furthermore, the bags cannot then be re-used.

By contrast, in the VERTI-GRO system each pot holds 4000cc of medium and 4 plants share a pot. There is plenty of medium for most root systems and the bottom of each pot prevents the weight of the medium resting on the medium below. Each is an individual and separate unit, equipped with 12 x 6mm drainage holes dotted across the bottom of the pot. The nutrient is allowed to trickle unimpeded from the top to the bottom of the stack and nutrient and oxygen supply is even and uninterrupted. Plant growth is therefore quite even as light, oxygen and nutrient are supplied and received evenly. The entire stack rests on the ground and is not suspended from the tunnel. Pots can be used over and over again.

Sadly, the numbers of people with gold or silver handshakes from retrenchments and willing to start a franchise has meant that the market has seen an entry of individuals not experienced or qualified in the Hydroponics world. They are easy targets for unscrupulous franchisors, who themselves, often lack technical expertise or knowledge of their subject. .

Plant quality is of the utmost importance in Hydroponics and any drop in quality of the plants supplied will have a direct effect on the yields experienced by the franchisee. Prospective franchisees should make absolutely sure that plants supplied by the franchisor have been properly grown and treated. If they comprise genetically modified material, franchisees should make quite sure that the plants are suitable for growth in the country for which they are destined. It's no good believing what the prospective seller tells you, you must find out for yourself. Remember the old adage here "If someone's trying to sell you something, don't believe a word he says". For example, if plants have been bred for growth in a cool, dry climate overseas, don't expect them to do well anywhere near near a coast that is warm and humid. If they have been bred for latitudes or countries far removed from those where it's intended they should grow, don't expect them to do well no matter what the franchisor tells you rather let someone else be the guinea pig, especially when they qualify their attestations with "they've been tried and tested for local conditions and proven successful."

HERE ARE SOME USEFUL DO'S AND DON'TS

(for use with vertical growing systems in tunnels - not a definitive list)

DO:
___

1. Level your ground sloping 1.5% for drainage and away from inclination in the other direction.
2. Face your tunnels North/South for even light distribution.
3. Check your water for impurities. Have it analyzed to see whether you'll need to adjust the nutrient feed. Municipal water is expensive. You might need a borehole.
4. Get the best quality covers available for light distribution. Then, the south sides of the columns will get reflected light and you won't have to revolve the stacks in winter.
5. Include Aluminet covers if you intend growing crops that prefer cool conditions.
6. Use the strongest possible galvanized steel structures to withstand the strongest winds. You can cost skimp elsewhere but not here. The last thing you need is spaghetti, even if you are insured. Remember that rogue winds appear from nowhere.
7. Get as many erection teams going at the same time to reduce the time taken to get started. Once you get the go-ahead you'll want yields as quickly as possible.
8. Learn from others' mistakes - you can save yourself time and money.
9. Study the principles of hydroponics and plant genetics if you haven't done it before. A course in hydroponics will save you a great deal of money in school fees.

10.   Introduce Trichoderma into the system - it'll keep fungus away and helps to promote rapid growth.

11. Install a UV light sterilizer to kill pathogens.

12. Keep chlorine/ides and ammonia to minimum levels. No sodium at all. These three are highly toxic to many plants especially strawberries.

13. Adjust your tunnel temperatures to the plant's requirements. Get a professional to calculate the cooling system required for the corresponding temperature. There are not many people able to do this. Plastic is expensive because you must keep cooling the tunnel down. Rather look at shade cloth if possible - it breathes naturally.

14. Keep your % Rh lower than 60% during the day.

15.   Make sure that your range of cultivars dovetails with your start-up date. It's no good getting a cultivar which bears from July - December if your start-up date is January. By "start-up" I mean when you expect the plants to start bearing fruit. That would strangle your cash-flow.

16. Wrap your feeder pipes with insulation. You will want to feed during the daytime and cannot do so if your pipes are hot. Alternatively paint them white using white LDPE or HDPE if you can get it.

17. Bury all visible pipes for cooling and protection from the sun. Mark underground pipes and cables with flags/pennants to prevent accidental damage.

18. Feed for at least 30 mins. continuously each time. This will help prevent salinity build-up (because effectively you wash through).

19. Put filters everywhere i.e. main line, wet walls, nutrient circuit.

20. Feed wet walls from both ends – you need maximum flow.

<u>DON'T:</u>

1. Don't be tempted to reinvent the wheel by experimenting with anything untried i.e. Tunnels, covers, media, etc. Go the tried and tested route - it'll save you money. Experimenting costs school fees.
2. Don't run your system for less than 30-minute periods or you'll get salinity build-up.
3. Don't use PVC conduit alone for stacks more than 5 high - it's too flexible. Don't use white cable ties - (they are not UV resistant): black only.
4. Don't use galvanized poles to support the stacks. Nutrient solution is both saline and acidic and will cause the zinc ions to sacrifice into the nutrient solution resulting in zinc toxicity.
5. Don't use an exotic medium in which to grow the plants You can't afford to experiment.   Using coir only will result in oxygen starvation. Vermiculite breaks down after a while, Perlite is expensive. Rather not re-invent the wheel but stick with the tried and trusted like composted pine bark. If you use the medium grade you will get ideal water retention and nutrient flow through. NB it MUST be composted to remove pathogens.
6. Don't use a nutrient mixture whose ammonia level (for nitrogen) is higher than 10%. 5% ammonia is about the level most suited to the plants' absorption capabilities.
7. Don't use any pyrethrums in your system - they kill "friends".
8. Don't use systemics – if the plants fruit all the time the fruit will be toxic if you do. Rather apply biologicals.

CHAPTER THIRTY –THREE
SAVE MONEY BY GROWING YOUR OWN VEGETABLES.

Everybody is acutely aware of the rising cost of living as it becomes more and more difficult with every passing month to keep expenses within one's budget. Petrol, electricity and food seem to be the main culprits behind this difficult situation.

The price of petrol is nearly at its highest level ever while the government slaps higher and higher levies onto the cost of fuel.

The third baddie in this triumvirate is food; successive minimum labour increases along with the cost of fuel has rocketed food prices to inflationary levels, and none of this has been helped by periodic droughts.

Now we may not be able to do much about the cost of electricity and fuel but we can do something about the high cost of food. Yet again, as with electricity, one has to somehow escape from the merry-go-round of continually enriching resellers by buying their produce. The resellers do very little in the way of active production. The farmer grows the produce requiring expertise and patience, exposing himself to risk of wipe-out by pests and diseases or Act of God and delivers his quality-controlled product to the reseller who then puts it on his shelf. The shopper takes it to the till point where they ching-ching up the sale and bank your payment.

Retailers generally mark-up produce by about 60% so if, for example, lettuces are selling at $1.00 each (which they generally do in the hot months as they are difficult to grown then and the demand is at its highest) then the farmer gets 0.62c for each lettuce and the retailer gets 0.37c. The farmer must deduct labour, diesel, electricity, fertiliser and overhead costs from his $0.62c, which account for about 60% of his turnover, leaving him with the same net profit as the retailer, and this when lettuces are in peak demand and at their highest price. In the cool months lettuces are easy to grow and the demand is suppressed due to the cool weather so the farmers' profit is even less.

You can remove yourself from this vicious circle by growing your own produce and capitalise on both the farmer's and the retailer's profits together, and if you grow hydroponically your costs will be lower than that of a farmer growing in soil. But in order to make your produce more economically attractive than that of the retailers you would have to offer your produce at a discounted price, say 15% lower than theirs.

Let's do the sums:

A 5 x 3m greenhouse equipped with a Verti-Gro vertical growing system houses 838 plants. Lettuces take an average of 5 weeks to mature in hydroponics so you should be able to get 10 crops a year from your greenhouse which is 8380 plants (take off 380 plants for accidents, pests and a less than 100% germination rate).

So 8000 plants sales at an average annual price of say $0.65 = $5200. At the outset a 15m2 greenhouse will cost you $1500 complete with weldmesh monkey excluder, a fibreglass roof, 60% shadecloth and white plastic floor sheeting, leaving $3700 gross profit from which you'd have to pay out for electricity, water and fertiliser costs. Two bags of water soluble fertiliser costing $25 will last you a year and a 25kw submersible pump switched on for 1.5 hours a day uses very little electricity. Estimate $40 per month for these expenses will leave you with a nett profit of $3200 for the year.

Of course you'd have to market your own produce too which is not easy in the beginning but once you've set up a channel of distribution it becomes a lot easier.

Now let's have a look at growing vegetables for your own home consumption. You will need to grow a spread of vegetables, planting a greater variety at lower quantities. The number of Verti-Gro columns will have to be reduced to a single row and in their place you can put two rows of bags from which you can grow peppers and egg plants. Cucumbers and tomatoes can be grown from the second pot in the vertical column leaving the top pot for your lettuces. (All seven lower pots are removed for this purpose and replaced with a white drainage pipe and a funnel. The tomato and cucumber plants grow outwards and downwards.

Although tomatoes, cucumbers. peppers and eggplants take up more space than the lettuces so you fit fewer in the green house, what they lack in quantity they make up for in value. Peppers sell for $3.35/kg in the shops. They produce at about 1 pepper per plant per month, so with 16 plants in a row of bags they would contribute 4 kg a month over 9 months = 36kg x $3.35 = **$121 p.a. saved.**

Tomatoes can be grown year round in a subtropical climate, producing 6 kg each a year from two crops x 64 plants = 6 x 64 = 384 kg x $1.25/kg = **$480 saved**. Cucumbers produce 10 kg fruit over 3 months x 2 crops per year = 20kg per plant p.a. Therefore a crop of 32 will produce = 640kg @ $1.65/kg = **$1056 saved.**

Eggplants produce two crops per year @ 1kg per plant = 2 kg per year x 32 plants = 64 kg x 4 fruits per kg = 256 fruits @ $0.65 each = **$165 saved**.
Lettuces: 320 lettuces p.a. @ average annual price $1.00/lettuce = **$320 saved.**
Total estimated savings p.a. = $2142 (Less cost of water, electricity, seed and fertilisers @ say $142 netting you **$2000 p.a. saved**. Alternatively, work out what you are actually spending on these items p.a. Any estimates will depend on individual consumption rates.

CHAPTER THIRTY-FOUR
THE 'BREATHING' GREENHOUSE CONCEPT

With the advent of plastics it has become fashionable to erect plastic covered greenhouses to grow produce, often at great expense because of the high cost of the metal that must be used to support the plastic.

Apart from the disproportionately high cost, plastic is not the right material to use in hot high humidity areas. The sun's rays penetrate the plastic (radiation) and the inside of the tunnel becomes intolerably hot. If water is used to cool the tunnel down then the resultant humidity level becomes unacceptably high for the plants. Transpiration cannot take place effectively and diseases, especially fungal diseases, proliferate. Often, the humidity can rise as high as 95%.

Even if no water cooling is used the moisture contained in the plants can contribute to a high humidity level with just the same outcome. No growth takes place at temperatures above 30°C.

Recommended Solution:

Seedling Growers have been using wooden poles and shade cloth since their very inception and still do to this day. Most often the method of growing is hydroponic which means that seedling growers have long chosen a system that most ideally suits the plants. Shade cloth is cool (varying occluding percentages can be used to suit the % shade cover desired) and allows air movement within the greenhouse which lowers humidity levels. Having established that plastic cannot be used on its own because of the heat we also need to recognize that shade cloth cannot be used on its own either because of its inability to keep neither plants nor the workers dry in wet weather. Therefore, the ideal solution is to have a combination of the two where plastic on the top can keep plants and workers dry but shade cloth on the sides can allow the tunnel to breathe. The most practical solution is to fit shade cloth from the clamp rail to the ground, leaving the ends of the tunnel open.

The Dual Parallel Feeding System:

Greenhouses can be built with gum poles and shade cloth to achieve maximum benefit from lower temperatures and air movement. In addition however, other materials are also used to achieve a cost effective method of growing fruit and vegetables.

Dual extruded PVC sheeting (black down, white up) is used to inhibit weeds and reflect as much available light within the greenhouse for the plants' use, without any heat being introduced into the growing area.

In addition and wherever possible, the Verti-Gro system is used which results in 6 times the number of plants being grown in the same area. Thus in a 100m2 greenhouse that could normally accommodate only 500 plants, with Verti-Gro it could accommodate 3 000 plants. This makes the operation highly cost-effective.

Under normal circumstances a mixture of fruits and vegetables cannot be grown in a single hydroponic greenhouse because each plant requires a different EC (Electrical Conductivity that measures the strength of the nutrient solution). By grouping certain veggies together one is able to arrive at two groups that can be fed two different EC nutrient solutions respectively, but in parallel. The nutrient solutions are kept separate throughout the feeding maze by means of two separate header tanks and separate feeding and drainage plumbing systems.

Time clocks are used to control the respective feeding times which can also be different when necessary.

Conclusion:

The net result is that 14 different types of veggies can be grown in say, a 72m2 greenhouse housing 546 plants which is almost 8 plants per m2. Aside from vertical growing, a variety of different growing systems such as gravel beds and bag culture are used to achieve this result.

In summary, plants are grown in a perfectly suitable environment, fed perfect nutrition in a cost-effective setting. With diligent pest and disease control management perfect yields can be expected.

Source: DaisyFresh Hydroponics

Wisdom occasionally pops up in the most surprising places. Just such an example which applies widely across the board including hydroponic enterprises is the following for which we must thank GOOGLE

TO REFLECT AND ACT

The difference between the poor countries and the rich ones is not the age of the country

This can be shown by countries like India & Egypt that are more than 2000 years old and are poor.

On the other hand, Canada, Australia & New Zealand, that 150 years ago were inexpressive, today are developed countries and are rich.

The difference between poor & rich countries does not reside in the available natural resources.

Japan has a limited territory, 80% mountainous, inadequate for agriculture and cattle raising, but it is the third world economy. The country is like an immense floating factory, importing raw material from the whole world and exporting manufactured products

Another example is Switzerland, which does not plant cocoa but has the best chocolate in the world. In its little territory they raise animals and plant the soil during only 4 months of the year. Not enough, they produce dairy products of the best quality. It is a small country that transmits an image of security, order and labour, which made it the world's strongest safe.

Executives from rich countries who communicate with their counterparts in poor countries show that there is no significant intellectual difference.

Race or skin colour is also not important: immigrants labelled lazy in their countries of origin are the productive power in rich European countries.

What is the difference then?
The difference lies in the attitude of the people, framed along the years by the education & the culture.

On analysing the behaviour of the people in rich & developed countries, we find that the great majority follow the following principles in their lives:

1. *Ethics, as a basic principle*
2. *Integrity*
3. *Responsibility*
4. *Respect of the laws & rules*
5. *Respect of the rights of other citizens*
6. *Work Loving*
7. *Strive for Saving & Investment*
8. *Will of super action*
9. *Punctuality*

In poor countries, only a minority follow these basic principles in their daily life

We are not poor because we lack natural resources or because nature was cruel to us.

We are poor because we lack the right attitude.

We lack the will to comply with and teach these functional principles of rich & developed societies.

ACKNOWLEDGEMENTS

Sources:

Much of the material contained in this book is taken from ACS Distance Learning, Stourbridge, UK and constituted the learning material for the Hydroponics courses 1, 2 and 3 which I studied and passed.

The balance of the intellectual information I drew from my own personal experience while owner-managing my strawberry farm during 2000 to 2010.

I'm indebted to Anthony Turton of Touchstone Resources for the maps and tables in the section on the world water shortage and saving water through hydroponics, and to my wife Jenny for her endless patience.

Individual graphs and photographs are acknowledged underneath each one.
NFT - p.37
© Kenishirotie | Dreamstime.com - <ahref="https://www.dreamstime.com/royalty-free-stock-image-hydroponic-vegetable-image31302426#res18197087">Hydroponic Vegetable Photo</a>

DWC - p.44
© Banprik | Dreamstime.com - <a href="https://www.dreamstime.com/stock-photo-hydroponics-vegetables-roots-water-vegetable-fresh-lettuce-growing-system-image64556523#res18197087">Hydroponics -vegetables Roots In Water Photo</a>

INDEX

withholding periods, 88, 90, 107
WOOD SHAVINGS, 70, 74
xylem, 12
yields, 5, 7, 8, 13, 20, 21, 26, 47, 48, 65, 110, 128, 155, 156, 160, 161, 170
Zinc, 18, 22, 128, 163

For all types of growing structures, specialising in multispans, contact:

For sales enquiries or orders for Verti-Gro products in Southern Africa please contact:

DaisyFresh Hydroponics
Marc Service
2 Bellows Road
Gordon's Bay
7140 Western Cape
Tel: +27(0) 76 627 7680
Email: servicemarc@gmail.com